D1248097

COURSE CONSTRUCTION IN
Industrial Arts
AND
Vocational Education

J. W. GIACHINO, Ed.D.
Professor of Industrial Education and
Head, Vocational-Industrial Education Department
Western Michigan College of Education
Kalamazoo, Michigan

RALPH O. GALLINGTON, Ed.D.
Acting Head, Applied Science
Professor of Industrial Education
Chairman of Industrial Education Department
Southern Illinois University
Carbondale, Illinois

AMERICAN TECHNICAL SOCIETY · CHICAGO ILLINOIS

PREFACE

At some time or other teachers of industrial arts and vocational education will be confronted with the task of preparing a course of study. If such a course of study is to have any value, it should be based on sound and practical principles of course construction.

Effective teaching is contingent on many factors, but unless a teacher is able to organize instructional material into worth-while educative experiences, many of these factors will lose their potentialities. Although a course of study is necessary for all instructional areas, it is of even greater significance in situations where manipulative processes are involved. For it is axiomatic that when learning deals with performance type of activities, some kind of an analysis is mandatory, otherwise it will be impossible to identify and assemble a core of essential and related work experiences which will affect the attainment of desired goals of achievement. Furthermore, manipulative operations require a certain sequential order of performance which means that the teachable content must have a logical and methodical manner of presentation.

The purpose of this book is to provide some of the more fundamental principles of writing a practical course of study. Since courses in industrial arts and vocational education have many things in common, even though their basic philosophies differ, the principles described will apply to both of these instructional areas. The material should be of considerable value to students majoring in industrial arts and vocational education as well as to teachers and administrators who are currently in the field and must of necessity continually prepare or revise their courses.

The practices presented in the text are the result of many years of experience in assisting students and teachers to plan and organize instructional activities for their classes. Actually the book represents the thinking of many individuals, and as it is difficult to acknowledge each by name, we merely extend our sincere gratitude to all who have made helpful contributions.

J. W. GIACHINO
RALPH O. GALLINGTON

CONTENTS

CHAPTER   PAGE

1. BASIC ELEMENTS OF AN INSTRUCTIONAL PLAN 1

2. DEFINITIONS OF INSTRUCTIONAL AREAS 12

3. MAJOR FACTORS INVOLVED IN DEVELOPING COURSE OF STUDY . 22

4. PREPARING THE INTRODUCTORY STATEMENT FOR A COURSE OF STUDY 28

5. FORMULATING A PLAN OF INSTRUCTIONAL PRACTICES 35

6. DEVELOPING A STATEMENT OF EDUCATIONAL PHILOSOPHY . . 48

7. ESTABLISHING SPECIFIC COURSE OBJECTIVES 61

8. THE INSTRUCTIONAL ANALYSIS 68

9. ANALYZING A COURSE FOR ITS BASIC OPERATIONS 72

10. ARRANGING OPERATIONS IN AN INSTRUCTIONAL ORDER . . . 78

11. SELECTING THE WORK JOBS AND PROJECTS 87

12. ANALYZING A COURSE FOR ITS RELATED INFORMATION . . . 95

13. ANALYZING OPERATIONS AND RELATED INFORMATION . . . 102

14. ASSEMBLING THE COURSE OF STUDY 109

15. INSTRUCTION SHEETS 121

16. STUDENT PLANNING 128

17. STUDENT STUDY GUIDES 135

CHAPTER 1

Basic Elements of an Instructional Plan

A sound educational plan is essential to the effective and efficient operation of any school system. An educational plan may be defined as any learning environment wherein adequate experiences are provided which permit pupils to develop their abilities to their maximum potentialities. Specifically, this means that boys and girls are given the opportunity to participate in worth-while educative activities that will enable them to become successful participants in a democratic society.

An adequate educational plan implies instructional organization. Without good organization, learning is likely to be haphazard and wander aimlessly over doubtful avenues of attainment. Actually, success in any field of endeavor hinges materially on the degree of organization established. Time and time again a business enterprise or a private venture has failed because of improper organization. Likewise, the success with which any school system can discharge its responsibilities depends considerably on how well it has organized its instructional program.

Although an instructional plan has many administrative and supervisory ramifications, basically it may be said to consist of the following components:

1. Program of studies
2. Curriculums
3. Courses of study

PROGRAM OF STUDIES

A program of studies represents the total offering of a school system. As such, it includes not only the school subjects, but all the extracurricular activities in which pupils may participate. Thus, the program of studies may comprise several curriculums such as college preparatory, general, commercial, industrial, agriculture, and homemaking.

Naturally, the more extensive the program of studies, the greater the services a school can render to its pupils. Schools with a limited program of studies must of necessity restrict their educational opportunities and thereby fail to provide a type of education that meets the needs of all youth. This becomes apparent immediately when the total program of a school includes only a college preparatory curriculum. Since such a curriculum is designed primarily for students planning to enter college, it cannot serve those who are not interested in or are unable to go to college. A high-school program of studies which emphasizes only the traditional college preparatory program is meeting the needs of only a small percentage of the high-school population. It is interesting to note that, according to a recent survey, for every 100 children entering the fifth grade, fewer than half graduate from high school and only about 38 out of 100 high-school graduates are currently entering college.

It is granted that a program limited in its scope of offering may possess the highest quality of instruction; nevertheless, when a program of this kind is appraised in terms of the pupils' needs, it must be considered ineffective. Accordingly, a school system, in addition to possessing capable teachers, adequate education facilities, and competent administrative and supervisory personnel, must have a program that will provide a wide variety of educational opportunities for students of varying interests and abilities.

CURRICULUMS

In reviewing the vast mass of educational literature, there will be found many concepts of the term curriculum. Some educational writers define it as a sequence of instructional units, while others say it is a systematic arrangement of courses designed for a particular group of pupils. The more current educational philosophy refers to the curriculum as a summation of all the experiences in which students are engaged under the direction of the school.

After a careful analysis of various definitions, it would seem safe to conclude that, in its broadest sense, a curriculum is an orderly arrangement of integrated subjects, activities, and experiences which students pursue for the attainment of a specific goal. In each case the learning involves the acquisition of knowledge, mastery of certain skills, and the development of desirable attitudes. The curriculum generally extends over a definite period of time and is usually designed for certain groups of students. For example, a college preparatory curriculum in a senior high school may consist of study in English, mathematics, physics, chemistry, history, etc., for a three-year period, for students whose specific objective is to prepare for college. A vocational curriculum in woodwork might appear as in Fig. 1.

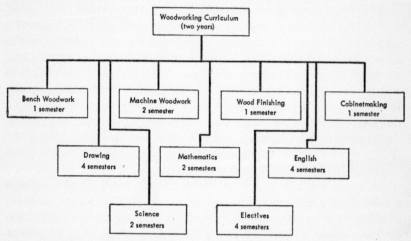

Fig. 1.   Diagram of a Vocational Curriculum in Woodwork

COURSE OF STUDY

There is probably no other device that more clearly reveals actual instructional practices in a school system than the course of study. Whereas the curriculum identifies the major areas of instructional activities, the course of study definitely specifies the means of achieving the specific experiences desired.

Various definitions of a course of study will be found. For example, Caswell and Campbell[1] define it as: ". . . a guide for teachers in the selection of pupil activities, the material to be used in connection with these activities, and the manner in which they are to be organized." Reeder[2] refers to it as: "That part of the curriculum which is organized for classroom." Ericson[3] describes a course of study as "A presentation of

---

[1] H. L. Caswell and D. S. Campbell, *Curriculum Development* (New York: American Book Company, 1935), p. 451.

[2] Ward G. Reeder, *A First Course in Education* (New York: The MacMillan Company, 1943), p. 354.

[3] E. E. Ericson, *Teaching the Industrial Arts* (Peoria, Ill.: Chas. A. Bennett Company, 1946), p. 286.

3

teaching material organized and arranged for instructional use. In its simplest form, it may consist of a mere outline of topics to be covered or processes to be performed. In more complete form, it will include additional features for the purpose of assisting the teacher in the presentation of the subject matter."

In essence, then, a course of study is a comprehensive plan which shows the scope and teaching sequence of all the activities provided for a particular subject in a curriculum. Just as there is need for planning a production job in industry, so, too, is planning regarded as indispensable for teaching any course. Industry would consider it ridiculous to attempt the fabrication of a product without first making detailed drawings and planning all the manufacturing operations. If planning is so important in transforming a raw material into a finished product, how much more important it is to plan judiciously the course of action needed to effect desirable learning attitudes in young people. A course of study represents careful planning; it is really the master blueprint of instruction.

IMPORTANCE OF A COURSE OF STUDY

Instruction, to be conducted properly, must proceed on some systematic basis. It is frequently stated that 50 per cent of good teaching is careful planning. The instructor who relies entirely on his memory, skimpy outlines, or day-to-day planning cannot possibly set up an educational environment that is conducive to good teaching. Lasting learning comes only when there is a logical presentation of learning activities—activities that have been thoroughly analyzed and selected on the basis of their functional value and ease of understanding. No instructor can possibly discharge his responsibilities without subjecting his course to some form of critical analysis. A careful analysis will permit him to select the information and skills which he wishes his students to acquire and to arrange this material in such a manner that learning progresses rapidly and effectively. The development of a course of study makes it possible for the teacher to think through his course and thereby form a clear picture of what he wants to get across to his students. It gives him an opportunity to appraise each activity, to add significant experiences, or to reject material that is inappropriate or doubtful in value.

The course of study also serves as a ledger wherein the instructor can record instructional changes periodically, as they may be desired. For example, if he finds that certain jobs or projects which he has included for a particular unit of work do not seem to be entirely satisfactory, he can make notations of this fact and provide suitable changes. When the course is repeated, the same mistakes will not be made. Very often, too, the alert teacher will discover some new technical information, process, or teaching device that may enrich a definite phase of the course. Without a course of study, he has to make a mental note of this data with the idea that he will use it at the appropriate time and place. Unfortunately, the lapse of time will probably dim his memory, and consequently the material may never be used. On the other hand, if there is a course of study, the instructor is more likely to make an entry of the information and actually use it at the suitable time.

NEED FOR CONTINUAL REVISION[4]

Once a course of study is completed, it is foolhardy for the instructor to assume that his task of course organization is done. If a course of study is to serve its intended purpose, it must not be looked upon as a stereotyped set of plans to be deposited on some shelf and forgotten. It is as dangerous to consider a course of study as a finished product as it is to attempt to teach without one.

Instructional conditions are subjected to frequent changes. New processes, materials, tools, and machinery may come into manufacturing existence. Perhaps some of the jobs, projects, or operations which seemed satisfactory at the time the analysis was made may in time prove inappropriate for the students. All of this means that the instructor must frequently examine his course of study and make such changes as are necessary to keep his instruction up to date. When instruction lags too far behind actual practices, it has lost its true significance whether it be industrial arts, homemaking, agriculture, technical, or trade. Outmoded practices cease to make instruction practical, and the recipients of this type of teaching are thereby deprived of meaningful experiences.

RESPONSIBILITY FOR PREPARING A COURSE OF STUDY

In past decades it was not an unusual practice for a teacher to be handed a course of study by a supervisor and told to follow it. Sometimes this course of study was one issued by the state department of public instruction, or perhaps it may have been prepared by the supervisor himself. The attempt to force a course of study on a teacher is just about as inconsistent as telling a teacher to teach machine shop when he has never had any training in this area. A course of study can never be prepared by an individual or a committee that is far removed from the ac-

---

[4] E. M. Bollinger and G. G. Weaver, *Occupational Instruction* (New York: Pitman Publishing Corporation, 1945), p. 135.

tual teaching scene with the expectation that its mandates will be carried out with any degree of success. To be of any value, a course of study must be "tailor made" to fit the individual teaching situation. Moreover, most teachers are inclined to resent the idea of following a set of plans which they have had no part in preparing.

Fortunately, the theory that construction of a course of study was in the province of the subject expert no longer is looked upon by school administrators as tenable. Current practices show that the teacher is being given more of this responsibility. Administrators have come to realize that the teacher who must use the material is in a much better position to prepare the course of study.[5]

It is logical for the teacher who is working under a supervisor to seek the advice and assistance of the supervisor when undertaking the preparation of a course of study.[6] Especially is this true if the teacher is to organize a course of study for the first time, or if he has to construct a course of study for a new subject. In each instance, the supervisor will be able to offer certain suggestions which unquestionably may prevent pitfalls later. Sometimes a supervisor in a large school system may appoint a committee of several teachers to work together in preparing a course of study if the same subject is taught by more than one teacher. A far better course of study will be produced through the combined judgment of several teachers than one written by any single individual.

Many teachers of industrial arts and vocational education have little or no direct supervision. Consequently, these people are often confronted with the problem of working alone. In such cases it is advisable for them to consult outside sources for assistance. One plan is to contact a teacher preparation institution. Usually someone at the college will be in a position to offer invaluable aid. Another possibility is for the teacher to consult members of the state department of education. Most state departments maintain consultants who can render expert assistance.

Meeting with men in industry, agriculture, or business should never be overlooked. Frequently, these people will welcome the opportunity to sit with the teacher and work out a suitable plan of instruction. Finally, the teacher can refer to courses of study prepared in other schools. Although such courses of study may not be entirely suitable for one's teach-

---

[5] H. R. Douglass, *The High School Curriculum* (New York: The Ronald Press Company, 1947), p. 323.

[6] E. E. Ericson, *Teaching the Industrial Arts* (Peoria, Ill.: Chas A. Bennett Company, 1946), p. 287.

ing situation, nevertheless, they may provide many ideas which can be incorporated into the course of study that is being written.

COURSE OUTLINE

A course of study should not be confused with a course outline. Whereas the former is a detailed plan of instruction, a course outline is merely a skeleton or topical outline of the material to be taught. The principal value of a course outline is that it quickly gives the school administrator a general idea of the content and scope of the subject to be covered. Since a superintendent, principal, or supervisor often maintains a file of the various subjects taught in the school system, the availability of a course outline is desirable. Another value of a course outline is that it frequently serves as a basis for preparing a course of study. Thus, an instructor may want to get a quick picture of the course before starting the detailed course of study. By having an outline, he will have a better perspective of the instructional material that is to be covered. Examples of partial course outlines will be found in this chapter.

PARTS OF A COURSE OF STUDY

A really comprehensive course of study should include the following information:

1. A general introductory statement specifying the main concepts of the course.
2. The grade level for which the course is intended.
3. The main divisions of the course, with a time limit for each.
4. Specific practices that are to be followed in teaching.
5. Philosophy and objectives pertaining to the specific area of instruction as well as course aims.
6. An orderly arrangement of the manipulative operations to be learned.
7. An outline of the essential related information.
8. The media to be used in learning the established skills and knowledge (projects, jobs, problems, etc.).
9. The activities which are designed especially to foster the development of desirable attitudes and good work habits.
10. The nature of instructional aids that will be used to simplify learning.

In subsequent chapters, each of the above-mentioned factors will be discussed in detail. Information also will be given on how to analyze a course and how the selected contents should be arranged in a logical teaching order.

EXAMPLE OF COURSE OUTLINE
FOR
AIRCRAFT CARBURETION AND LUBRICATION

COURSE OUTLINE

Title of Course: "Aircraft Carburetion and Lubrication"

Length of Course: One semester—72 hours

Objective of Course: To give students an opportunity to:

1. Obtain a comprehensive knowledge of the various carburetion, fuel, and oil systems.

2. Master the basic skills in trouble shooting and maintenance of carburetors, fuel systems, and oil systems.

Divisions of Instruction

Phase   I. Carburetion.....................8 weeks
Phase II. Fuels and fuel systems..........4 weeks
Phase III. Lubricants and lubrication
           systems........................6 weeks

Phase I

Carburetion.........................8 weeks

Related Information

  A. Float type carburetors

    1. Function of the carburetor

    2. Fuel-air ratio
       a) Full-throttle
       b) Cruising
       c) Idling

    3. Functions of carburetor units
       a) Float and needle valve
       b) Discharge nozzle

   c) Air bleed
   d) Venturi
   e) Throttle valve
   f) Metering jets

  4. Carburetor accessories
   a) Mixture of altitude control
   b) Accelerating systems
   c) Economizers

  5. Operation
   a) Idling
   b) Accelerating
   c) Cruising
   d) Full-throttle

B. Diaphragm carburetors

  1. Construction
  2. Operation
   a) Idling
   b) Accelerating
   c) Cruising
   d) Full-throttle

C. Injection carburetors

  1. Construction
  2. Units of injection carburetors
  3. Functioning of injection carburetors
   a) Idling
   b) Accelerating
   c) Cruising
   d) Full-throttle
  4. Installation and adjustment of injection
   carburetors

D. Fuel injection

  1. Construction
  2. Function of fuel-injector units
  3. Installation and adjustments

Shop Work

Clean, inspect, assemble, and test various types
of aircraft carburetors.

EXAMPLE OF A COURSE OUTLINE
FOR
CLOTHING

COURSE OUTLINE

Title of Course: "Clothing"

Length of Course: One semester

Objective of Course: The purpose of this course is to direct high-school girls in a study of clothing problems. It provides specific experiences in planning and making simple garments.

Unit 1. Using a sewing machine

1. Starting and stopping
2. Threading
3. Straight stitching
4. Curved stitching
5. Oiling and cleaning machine

Unit 2. Hand sewing

1. Running stitch
2. Slant hemming

Unit 3. Making simple garments

1. Patterns
2. Getting ready to cut
3. Cutting out the garment
4. Assembling

Unit 4. Selecting fabrics for dresses

1. Types of dress fabrics
2. How fabrics are made
3. Why fabrics differ in price
4. Selecting the right fabric

Unit 5. Making and fitting a dress

1. Preparing working plan
2. The first fitting
3. How to judge the fit of a dress
4. Second fitting
5. Final fitting
6. Finishing and pressing the dress

Unit 6. Altering and remaking dresses
1. How a dress should be altered
2. Simple altering
3. Remaking a dress

DISCUSSION QUESTIONS:

1. Why is good organization so essential for effective instruction?
2. What is meant by a program of studies?
3. How does a limited program of studies contribute to an excessive number of students dropping out of school?
4. What type of a program of studies would be necessary to meet more adequately the needs of secondary school youth?
5. What do we mean by a course of study?
6. What do we mean by a curriculum?
7. Cite several reasons why all teachers need a course of study.
8. Why is it important for the teacher to revise his course of study periodically?
9. What are the objections to following a course of study prepared by someone else?
10. What assistance should a teacher seek when preparing a course of study?
11. What is the difference between a course outline and a course of study?
12. Of what particular value is a course outline?

ADDITIONAL READING

Bollinger, E. W., and Weaver, G. G., *Occupational Instruction* (New York: Pitman, 1945), chap. I.

Caswell, H. L., and Campbell, D. S., *Curriculum Development* (New York: American Book Company, 1935), chap. 16.

Douglass, H. R., *The High School Curriculum* (New York: Ronald Press, 1947), chap. 15.

Draper, E. M., *Principles and Techniques of Curriculum Making* (New York: D. Appleton-Century Company, 1936), chap. I.

Krug, E. A., *Curriculum Planning* (New York: Harper and Brothers, 1950), chap. I.

Paine, H. W., "Practical Nomenclature in the Fields of Vocational Curriculum Construction," *Industrial Arts and Vocational Education*, November, 1945, p. 383.

Spears, Harold, *The Teacher and Curriculum Planning* (New York: Prentice-Hall, 1951).

CHAPTER 2

Definitions of Instructional Areas

Definitions of instructional areas may appear somewhat extraneous in a text dealing with the preparation of a course of study, but their inclusion is justified for the following reasons:

1. Due to the many segments of vocational and practical arts education, teachers often have only hazy ideas as to the function of these programs. Since all instructional areas are important facets of the total educational program for youth, teachers should, in addition to their own field of specialty, be familiar with other aspects of education if they are to discharge their responsibilities realistically and intelligently.
2. By having clear concepts of other areas of education, teachers can usually organize their own instructional material better.
3. Misconception of the function and value of various phases of an educational program is often the result of a misunderstanding of the meaning of basic educational terminology.

The purpose of this chapter is not to present lengthy discussions of all the implications of education, but rather to define briefly those educational programs that have some relationship to industrial arts and vocational education.

GENERAL EDUCATION

Many detailed definitions of general education have been written, but essentially general education refers to the:

1. Experiences provided to develop the native capacities of youth to their fullest extent.

2. Learning process that brings about a development of the intellectual, physical, and emotional qualities of children so they may grow into useful and intelligent citizens.
3. Educative program that provides the environment, the opportunity, and the guidance for the attainment of those patterns of behavior that satisfy the needs of the child and society.

In its broadest sense, general education includes all the curricular and extracurricular activities offered by a school system in order that human beings may acquire the essential skills, knowledge, and attitudes demanded by their social environment. Specifically, general education is designed to develop functional understandings of essential elements of life and society which people must possess to live normal and happy lives.

INDUSTRIAL ARTS

Industrial arts is a phase of general education in which the primary purposes are to familiarize students with the tools, products, processes, and occupations of industry as well as the social and economic phenomena of the technological world in which they live and work. It is considered a part of general education, not only because it supports or fulfills many of the fundamental concepts of general education, but because it develops greater understandings of the significance of industry in the world of today. Since industry is an element of our basic culture, industrial arts, therefore, assumes the responsibility of enhancing and enriching the experiences of young people in this important phase of our industrial world.

PRACTICAL ARTS

Practical arts is a phase of general education concerned with such physical work as is done in the home, industry, agriculture, business, and the arts. The emphasis in these areas is not on occupational competency, as in vocational education, but on an understanding of their relationship to successful living. (Industrial arts is considered a part of the practical arts program.) This phase deals with work that is generally performed by most people. According to Fales,[1] "Practical arts is represented in the school by easels, workbenches, tools, typewriters, accounts, business correspondence, musical instruments, flowers, pets, furniture, automobiles, radios, books, clothing, the preparation and preservation of foods, and

[1] Roy G. Fales, "The Role of Practical Arts Education," *School Shop*, November, 1948, p. 5.

13

the work of the home. These types of school work are usually found in shops, home economics rooms, fine arts rooms, commercial rooms, and agricultural laboratories."

VOCATIONAL EDUCATION

"Vocational Education" is a generic term embracing all the experiences an individual needs to prepare for some useful occupation. As defined in the "Statement of Policies for the Administration of Vocational Education," the purpose of vocational education is to provide training, to develop skills, abilities, understandings, attitudes, working habits, and appreciations, and to impart knowledge and information needed by workers to enter and make progress in employment on a useful and productive basis.[2]

Although the term vocational education has no limits as to types of occupations, it generally excludes the professions. It is used here to apply specifically to useful employment in trades and industry, agriculture, homemaking, technical, and business areas. Such programs may or may not be federally subsidized. When certain requirements are met, reimbursement is possible through the Smith-Hughes and George-Barden Acts.

VOCATIONAL-INDUSTRIAL EDUCATION[3]

Vocational-industrial education, which is frequently referred to as *trade and industrial education*, is a phase of vocational education that provides instruction in the development of basic manipulative skills, safety judgment, technical knowledge, and related industrial information for the purpose of fitting persons for useful employment in trades and industrial pursuits. The three main categories of training specified for a federally reimbursed program are: all-day trade, evening trade extension, and part-time.

1. **All-Day Trade Classes:** These classes are intended for persons enrolled in a full-time school who have selected a definite trade or industrial occupation and wish to prepare themselves for useful employment in that pursuit. To meet requirements for reimbursement, such classes must be limited to students who are fourteen years of age or over; they must be taught by occupationally qualified instructors, and classes must be in session for not less than nine months a year and thirty hours per

---

[2] Statement of Policies for the Administration of Vocational Education, Bulletin No. 1, U.S. Office of Education, Washington, D.C., p. 1.

[3] *Ibid.*, pp. 61–73.

week. All-day trade classes are divided into the following three groups:

Type A—Pupils in this course must spend one-half of the school day, amounting to not less than three consecutive clock hours per day or fifteen clock hours per week, in practical shop work. The remaining half day may be devoted to specified general education courses such as English, social studies, etc. However, a portion of this time, usually five hours per week, must be spent on related instruction having a direct functional value in the trade or occupation for which training is being given.

Type B—Classes of this type are similar to A except for the method of providing instruction in related subjects. In type B classes, the related instruction need not be taught in segregated classes as in type A, but may be given by the shop teacher as the need for it arises in shop work.

Type C—This is a special type of pre-employment trade training for persons eighteen years of age or for those who have legally left the full-time day school. The primary purpose of these classes is to provide intensive instruction for a specific single-purpose job such as a lathe operator, drill press operator, sheet metal riveter, etc. These courses may be conducted for any period of time without meeting the requirements as established for type A and B classes.

When instruction in an all-day trade class (either type A or B) is confined to preparation for a single trade or occupation such as machinist, welder, draftsman, electrician, etc., the course is referred to as a unit trade course. In communities having a population of 25,000 or less, where unit trade classes are not feasible, the all-day trade program may be organized to furnish instruction in a variety of related trades and industrial occupations. When organized on this basis, it is known as a general industrial course. Thus, the shop may be planned to offer training in bricklaying, plastering, painting, and cement work. Each student is permitted to specialize in one or more of these areas.

2. **Evening Trade Extension Classes:** The purpose of these classes is to provide the necessary instruction in trade skills and knowledge to increase the occupational efficiency of the worker in the trade or industrial pursuit in which he is employed or has been employed. These classes are usually held in the evening but may be conducted at any time when it is convenient for those enrolled.

3. **Part-Time Classes:** Part-time classes are intended for workers who return to school during a certain period of their regular working day. In the field of trade and industrial education there are three types of part-time classes. These are known as part-time trade extension, part-time trade preparatory, and part-time general continuation.

Part-Time Trade Extension instruction is for employed workers who are in need of additional skill and knowledge in the trade or occupation in which they are engaged. Unlike the evening trade extension classes, part-time trade extension instruction must be given during the regular school day and a co-operative arrangement must be made between employers and school officials for workers to receive such instruction. One plan of instruction is for apprentices who acquire the manipulative skills on the job, but return to school for related occupational instruction, such as blueprint reading, trade mathematics, science, workmen's compensation, and other similar subjects that are directly related to the occupations in which they are engaged. Another type is the co-operative program, usually called diversified occupations, whereby students spend half a day on the job and the remaining half day in regular high-school subjects and subjects related to their occupations.

Part-Time Trade Preparatory training is chiefly for persons who are employed and wish to prepare for a different industrial occupation. Due to the part-time character of this instruction, it cannot do more than provide the minimum knowledge and skills needed for beginning semiskilled industrial jobs.

Part-Time General Continuation classes were originally organized for out-of-school youth between the ages of fourteen and sixteen to enlarge their civic and vocational intelligence. These classes were designed primarily to satisfy state compulsory education laws, and instruction could cover any range of subjects that would enable young workers to discharge their responsibilities as citizens. Due to the many changes in the economic life of this nation since the inception of the Smith-Hughes Act, particularly federal and state child labor regulations and compulsory full-time school attendance to age sixteen, a great many of these classes and schools have been eliminated. Part-time continuation programs are now intended for workers above the compulsory school age who wish to take advantage of increasing their educational needs.

VOCATIONAL-TECHNICAL EDUCATION

The term "vocational-technical education" is used to denote preparation for a group of occupations which lie somewhere between the professions and skilled trades. This category of jobs demands less technical knowledge than is needed by a trained engineer or scientist and less manipulative competency than is required by the skilled mechanic. Whereas trade training emphasizes the mastery of manipulative skills with an understanding of technical knowledge, vocational-technical education places greater stress on laws of science and technical knowledge and their application to specific skills involved.

The product of vocational-technical education is technicians such as draftsmen, laboratory assistants, operators of highly technical equipment, production supervisors, and technical salesmen.[4]

INDUSTRIAL EDUCATION

Industrial education is a broad term that includes all educational activities dealing with modern industry. It is an inclusive term used when referring to industrial arts and vocational-industrial education.

VOCATIONAL-AGRICULTURAL EDUCATION[5]

The primary function of vocational-agricultural education is to assist people to become more proficient in farming. The program provides opportunities for persons who wish to acquire the necessary information and skills in operating and managing a farm and in helping those who are already established to improve their efficiency in farming operations.

Reimbursement is provided for classes organized on the following basis:

1. **All-Day Class:** An all-day class is one which is organized in a secondary school for students who wish to secure systematic training in agriculture. Instruction must be provided by a teacher who is qualified in agriculture by both special training and practical experience. Sufficient school time must be provided to allow for class, laboratory, and farmshop instruction as well as studies and observations in the field.

2. **Day-Unit Class:** A day-unit class is one that is planned to meet the needs of youth desiring agricultural instruction as a foundation for farming, but who are not classified or enrolled in a grade that is served by an all-day program in that school. Future Farmers of America or New Farmers of America activities are generally accepted as part of the instructional program. A day-unit class must meet for at least 90 consecutive minutes per class period per week throughout the regular school year and not less than one year of instruction in vocational agriculture must be offered.

3. **Classes for Young Farmers:** Young farmers' classes are designed to meet the needs of young men who are establishing themselves in farm-

[4] Vocational-Technical Training for Industrial Occupations, Bulletin No. 228, Washington, D.C., 1944, p. 1.

[5] Statement of Policies for the Administration of Vocational Education, Bulletin No. 1, U.S. Office of Education, Washington, D.C., pp. 38–44.

ing occupations. The instruction in these classes is planned so that it will serve youth who are legally out of school and who may not have had previous instruction in vocational agriculture. Classes of this type must provide supervised farm practices for each individual. There must be not less than fifteen class meetings each year for at least two years or the program may be conducted over the entire twelve-month span for a total of not less than thirty hours.

4. **Adult Farmer Classes:** Adult farmer classes are planned to assist adult farmers by developing their ability to solve their specific farming problems. There must be not less than ten meetings totaling at least twenty hours, over a period of not less than two weeks in any one year.

VOCATIONAL-HOMEMAKING EDUCATION[6]

The controlling purpose of vocational-homemaking is to provide instruction which will enable families to improve the quality of their family life through more efficient development and use of human and material resources. The program is designed to help the individual to live a more useful and satisfying personal, family, and community life. It deals specifically with financial planning, management of time and energy, human relationships, mechanics of housekeeping, and the utilization of technological developments in the home.

Three main categories of training are permissible under a federally reimbursed program. These are:

1. **All-Day School Program:** This program must be designed to meet the needs of persons fourteen years of age or over who are sufficiently mature to develop a realization of the importance of homemaking. The program is two years in length and should cover the major areas concerning food, clothing, shelter and people. Homemaking classes must meet for specified periods, the minimum time of which varies, depending on the conditions under which the program is operating. If the class is reimbursed from George-Barden funds the class must not be less than that required for a full unit of credit for other school subjects in the local school. When Smith-Hughes funds are used the class must meet for fifteen hours per week, except in cities under 25,000 population, in which case the time given to homemaking may not be less than one-half of the time per week for which the school is in session.

2. **Part-Time Programs:** Part-time programs are for youth fourteen years of age or over who have left the full-day school and wish short

[6] *Ibid.*, pp. 50–60.

courses in various homemaking areas. Instruction must be conducted for not less than 144 hours during the year.

3. Evening Classes: These classes are for people sixteen years of age or over who wish specific instruction dealing with one or more areas of home and family living. As a rule these classes meet for a minimum of two hours weekly for a sufficient number of meetings to achieve the purposes of the course.

VOCATIONAL-BUSINESS EDUCATION[7]

Vocational-business education is concerned with equipping both youth and adults with those skills and knowledge which will enable them to enter into or advance themselves in certain phases of employment in business. Federal reimbursement is possible for only those classes which provide instruction in distributive occupations. Instruction for these occupations may be organized on an evening basis for groups that are regularly employed in distributive occupations. Part-time classes may also be established for students who are working in distributive occupations or who contemplate entrance into this field. When enrolled in part-time classes, students must return to the regular day school for a prescribed number of hours each week.

Distributive Education refers to programs designed for persons sixteen years or over who are planning to enter occupations that are directly engaged in merchandising activities, or in contact with buyers and sellers when:

1. Distributing to consumers, retailers, jobbers, wholesalers, and others, the products of farm and industry, or selling services.
2. Managing, operating or conducting a retail, wholesale, or service business.

DIVERSIFIED OCCUPATIONS[8]

"Diversified Occupations" is a co-operative educational program for boys and girls sixteen years of age and over. This program provides systematic and supervised occupational training while employed in an industrial or business establishment. When enrolled in such a program, students spend one-half day on the job and the other half day in school. While on the job they learn the specific skills of the occupation. Their school time is devoted to prescribed high-school courses, a portion of

[7] *Ibid.*, pp. 45–49.
[8] *Ibid.*, pp. 67–68.

which must deal specifically with instruction related to the occupation in which they are engaged.

A diversified occupation program is particularly adaptable for communities where all-day type of classes cannot be justified.

DISCUSSION QUESTIONS

1. What are some of the activities of a school system that might be labeled general education?
2. How does general education differ from specialized education?
3. Why is industrial arts considered a phase of general education?
4. What is the difference between vocational education and vocational-industrial education?
5. What are the things that differentiate industrial arts from vocational-industrial education?
6. What is meant by practical arts education? Why is this phase a part of general education?
7. What is meant by industrial education?
8. Why should industrial arts be considered a part of a practical arts program?
9. What is meant by vocational-technical education? How can a vocational-technical education program be distinguished from an all-day trade preparatory program?
10. What are some of the general requirements for an all-day trade class?
11. What is the difference between a type A, B, and C all-day trade program?
12. What is the difference between a unit trade and a general industrial class?
13. What is meant by an evening trade extension class?
14. What are the three principal types of part-time classes? Explain the purpose of each type.
15. What is the primary function of vocational-agricultural education?
16. What type of classes may be provided in a federally reimbursed vocational-agricultural program?
17. In what way does a vocational-homemaking class differ from homemaking classes offered on a practical arts basis?
18. What type of classes may be provided in a federally reimbursed vocational-homemaking program?
19. What is the purpose of vocational-business education?
20. What is meant by distributive education?
21. What is the function of a diversified occupations program?

ADDITIONAL READING

Vocational Education for Youth, American Vocational Association, 1949.

Fales, Roy G., "The Role of Practical Arts Education," *School Shop,* November, 1948, p. 5.

Fern, George H., *What Is Vocational Education* (Chicago: American Technical Society, 1944), chap. 1.

Industrial Arts—Its Interpretation in American Schools, Bulletin No. 34, U.S. Office of Education, Washington, D.C., 1949, chap. 1.

Statement of Policies for the Administration of Vocational Education, Bulletin No. 1, U.S. Office of Education, Washington, D.C.

Technical Training for Industrial Occupations, Bulletin No. 228, 1944, U.S. Office of Education, Washington, D.C.

McCarthy, John., *Vocational Education: America's Greatest Resource* (Chicago: American Technical Society, 1950), chap. 6.

Mays, Arthur B., *Principles and Practices of Vocational Education* (New York: McGraw-Hill, 1948), chap. 1.

Mays, Arthur B., *Essentials of Industrial Education* (New York: McGraw-Hill, 1952), chaps. 9, 10, 11, 14.

Novak, Benjamin J., "What's Your Professional I.Q.?" Industrial Arts and Vocational Education, March, 1952, p. 104.

Prosser, Charles A., and Quigley, Thomas H., *Vocational Education in a Democracy* (Chicago: American Technical Society, 1949), chap. 1.

Reeder, Ward G., *A First Course in Education* (New York: Macmillan, 1943), chap. 1.

Struck, F. Theodore, *Vocational Education for a Changing World* (New York: John Wiley & Sons, 1945), chaps. 1, 2, 3, 12.

CHAPTER 3

Major Factors Involved in Developing a Course of Study

Success in developing a functional course of study is contingent on several factors, the most important of which are:

1. Extensive knowledge of the subject
2. Possession of a sound educational philosophy
3. Knowledge of the fundamental laws of learning
4. Understanding of basic teaching techniques

KNOWLEDGE OF SUBJECT

In order to prepare a comprehensive and practical plan of instruction, a teacher must, first of all, have an excellent understanding of his subject. Without an extensive background he will find it difficult to select, with any degree of success, the necessary material that will be appropriate for proper instruction. Industrial arts and vocational education courses deal with experiences involving manipulative operations; consequently, these teachers must have had, in addition to formalized training, some practical work experience. Such experience is mandatory for a teacher of vocational subjects because occupational competency can only be gained under the tutelage of one who has had first-hand contact with actual work. The industrial arts teacher, too, needs some practical experience even though it may not be of the same magnitude as that of the vocational teacher. Although the industrial arts teacher is not necessarily concerned with the development of high degrees of skill, nevertheless, one of his objectives is to interpret correctly industrial practices and technical knowledge to his students. This can be done only if he has had some practical work experience.

EDUCATIONAL PHILOSOPHY

A writer of a course of study must have acquired a sound philosophy of education—a philosophy that embraces his particular field of specialty as well as clear concepts of general education. Not only must the teacher understand the purpose of general education, but he must also know what contributions his subject area can make toward the implementation of the over-all educational philosophy. It is inevitable that without a working philosophy there can be no well-defined goals or objectives, and, without objectives, instruction is not likely to be free from encumbrances or be discerning enough to give instruction meaning and value. Effective teaching and learning, therefore, requires the establishment of purposeful objectives. Obviously, then, these objectives serve as a foundation upon which the course of study is constructed.

PRINCIPLES OF LEARNING

A teacher may have a well-defined philosophy of education but, unless he has an understanding of the basic principles of learning, he will experience difficulty in having students grow in terms of the established philosophy. These principles of learning will have to be reflected in the course of study; otherwise, it is impossible to arrange instructional activities into any logical teaching order. For example, a teacher must be aware of the fact that some things are easy to learn, while others are more difficult to master. Furthermore, certain types of information are retained with a greater degree of accuracy when properly related or associated with other factors, and failure to learn is often the result of improper orientation.

It is not the purpose here to discuss in detail all the important psychological principles of learning or how they should be infused in a course of study, but merely to indicate the importance of keeping these principles constantly in mind during the process of constructing a course of study. A few of the more basic learning principles that are particularly applicable to learning situations in industrial arts and vocational education are briefly summarized below.

1. **Best learning results when there is some means of applying what we learn.** In industrial arts and vocational education subjects, application of learning is held very high in the list of methods and techniques employed. Abstract thinking is held to a minimum, and any plan of in-

struction should give consideration to this important principle of learn-ing. If reading assignments are made, or if problem solving is being taught, it is best always to bring in some practical application which will give meaning and justification to the learning.

2. **We learn more readily when we are ready to learn or have a strong purpose or desire to learn.** Needs, purposes, and interests of students are often overlooked in planning instruction. It is always necessary to study carefully the individual student's readiness for learning, and to work with him individually in order that he will be able to participate more satisfactorily in the group lessons to follow.

3. **Learning is simplified if what we are learning is built on something we already know.** No two persons have exactly the same concepts of known facts or practices, but reference to the generally known is always an asset in planning a lesson or a course of study. Association of ideas helps students not only to attain new understandings, but it provides them with associations valuable in retaining the newly learned. Every new lesson should have some reference to the student's past experience.

4. **Learning to be effective must proceed in a logical order.** Some-times the logical order is from the more elementary or less difficult to the more advanced or more difficult, but there are occasions when the more basic learning is not the less difficult. Educators today give more emphasis to arranging learning units from the more basic to the more specialized. This emphasizes that the most basic learning enhances the learning which follows. When elementary or less difficult learning is cou-pled with basic learning, the process is much more satisfactory to pupil and teacher.

5. **Learning is problem-solving, and problems must be challenging to stimulate learning.** Too often a teacher is prone to solve all problems for the student by giving him too explicit directions. If the student is to learn at the maximum speed, he should have challenging problems thrown in his path. These problems must be within his ability and their solution must provide progress toward the goal he has set for himself. In solving problems, the student can mark his progress and derive memo-rable satisfactions from his efforts.

6. **More effective learning takes place when learning impressions come through more than one of the senses.** Seeing and hearing have come to represent the most used senses in our modern scheme of educa-tion. In industrial arts and vocational education classes, the student is able to learn a great deal through the senses of touch and smell, espe-cially the former. All senses should be used and developed. Recently, the

sixth sense, known as the kinesthetic sense, has become very important to these fields. The development of this sense is in reality a development of all the other senses, plus the perception of and physical awareness to all things in one's habitat. This development allows one to perform many tasks correctly and safely among people and things. Further, it decreases "accident proneness" in an individual and provides him with a feeling of security as he works.

7. **The first learning impressions are usually the most lasting; therefore, it is important not to convey wrong impressions which must be corrected later.** The lesson plan, and more remotely the course plan, will include motivating and interesting introductions to new material. All illustrations and introductions should be checked for: (1) appropriateness, (2) correctness, and (3) logical order. The student should be able to see the connection between the introductions and the main learning unit which follows. Conversely, he should not be wondering "what it is all about."

8. **Learning is more likely to take place if students have a reasonable chance of achieving early success in their endeavors.** Any assignment or project which has little to offer in the way of gradual and measurable progress may be questioned. Short assignments and smaller projects are best for beginners. The length will depend on the age and maturity of the students. Generally, younger or less mature students will require shorter assignments and smaller projects with marked and obvious levels of accomplishment.

9. **Feelings and emotions are strong incentives for learning.** Accomplishment may have a great deal to do with the development of an inferiority complex. Certain feelings and emotions may cause a student to develop such a complex also. It may be formed as a result of something the teacher has said or done unknowingly. Any good teacher should talk frequently with each student. It is only through constant contact that a teacher can determine what the student feels and what problems are hindering his progress.

10. **The most effective learning results when there is an immediate application of what is taught.** This is usually a very small problem with vocational and industrial arts teachers, because the teacher usually prepares his lessons and demonstrations slightly in advance of the students' needs. Each student immediately applies the lesson to his own work. All technical and related information should be co-ordinated with the practical work, thereby giving better understanding to the pupil as he associates it with his immediate tasks.

11. **The more often we use what we have learned, the longer we retain what is learned.** Instructional material should be organized to provide application of knowledge and skill. Learning a skill is very little different from learning a new fact. The more we recall a fact we have learned, the more likely it will become permanent knowledge. Likewise, the more we practice a skill, the more likely it will be retained as a skill.

12. **Learning requires motivation since interest is necessary for effective learning.** If we see a purpose or a need for what we are learning, the better will we retain what we are learning. The significant point to remember is that all students have needs around which purposes can be established. The teacher must discover these and make them known to the student in order that he may purposefully plan his learning with the teacher.

TEACHING TECHNIQUES

Besides having an understanding of the principles of learning, the successful teacher must know how to apply these principles. Too often a teacher is under the illusion that he is teaching, when in reality he is simply dispensing unrelated and factual information. Learning to be effective requires activity, and the teacher must provide wholesome experiences that result in purposeful activity. In developing a course of study, the teacher must anticipate certain desirable student outcomes and then must chart definite means by which these objectives will be attained. Success in such an endeavor necessitates a knowledge of teaching techniques which, in essence, refer to an understanding of five basic elements:

1. Methods to be used in teaching (demonstration, lecture, discussion, etc.).
2. Selection and organization of suitable instructional material (operation, related information, etc.).
3. Establishing practical activities as the media of instruction (projects, jobs, investigations, reports, experiments, etc.).
4. Method of evaluating pupil achievement and pupil growth.
5. Use of suitable teaching aids.

Since a course of study should include all of these elements, a teacher will be confronted with the problem of making many decisions such as how much detail he needs to include in his instructional plan, how he can best meet individual pupil needs, what work assignment will have functional values, and what devices will help vitalize his teaching. He will have to analyze an operation and decide if it can be taught, or if a specific activity is appropriate to attain a desirable goal. In short, the teacher will be required to use a type of judgment that is discriminating and sound—a judgment that demonstrates evidence of maturity, experience, and an understanding of teaching techniques.

DISCUSSION QUESTIONS

1. Why would a teacher have difficulty in setting up a suitable teaching environment if he lacked practical experience?
2. What would be some of the limitations of a course of study prepared by one lacking a sound working philosophy of education?
3. Why should principles of learning be taken into consideration when preparing a course of study?
4. What are some of the factors that contribute to effective learning?
5. One of the chief functions of a teacher is to instill in the student a desire to learn. How can this be done?
6. What are some of the specific ways in which sustained interest may be maintained?
7. Are Thorndike's three laws of learning still considered valid in terms of what we currently know of human behavior? What are these laws of learning? Show by actual examples how they affect learning.
8. What are some of the specific methods used in teaching?
9. Why is evaluation an important aspect of teaching?

ADDITIONAL READING

Fryklund, Verne C., *Trade and Job Analysis* (Milwaukee, Wis.: Bruce Publishing Company, 1947), chap. 10.

Jackey, David F., and Barlow, Melvin L., *The Craftsman Prepares To Teach*, Macmillan Company, 1944, chaps. 8, 10.

Leighbody, Gerald B., *Methods of Teaching Industrial Subjects* (Albany, N.Y.: Delmar, 1946), chap. 1.

CHAPTER 4 ————————————

Preparing the Introductory Statement for a Course of Study

The preparation of a course of study is an arduous and time-consuming task, yet the teacher will derive a great deal of satisfaction as he sees the results of his thinking and planning transformed into a product of reality. Just as the craftsman receives considerable pleasure in creating a finished article from raw material, so, too, will the conscientious teacher take pride in an achievement that will be highly instrumental in making learning effective.

The primary purpose of this chapter is to furnish the instruction necessary to prepare the first phase of the course of study, namely, the introduction.

INTRODUCTORY STATEMENT

The first section of any course of study should consist of a statement that clearly defines the nature of the course. This statement is comparable to the preface of a book or prologue of a play, since it sets the stage of events to follow. Anyone examining such a statement immediately should get an over-all view of what the teacher expects to accomplish. Perhaps even more significant, the introductory statement establishes certain conditions which limit the course of study to specific bounds and thereby provide a guide for the type of information, experiences, and activities to be included.

WHAT THE INTRODUCTORY STATEMENT SHOULD INCLUDE

The introductory statement should be expressed in terms of four conditions. They are:

1. The nature and degree of skill which students will be expected to master.
2. The nature of the related information to be studied.
3. The development of desirable attitudes.
4. The length, grade level, and entrance requirements of the course.

The first part of the statement should include the main areas of instruction to be covered. For example, if a course of study for an industrial arts general shop is to be written, the introduction might begin by mentioning that instruction will cover activities in wood, metal, drawing, electricity, and so on. If the course of study is to be planned for machine shop, the statement might stipulate that experience will be provided in running a lathe, milling machine, shaper and drill press. The introduction for a course in foods may indicate that study will involve menu planning, marketing, preparing and serving meals for the family. It will be noticed that in each of the examples mentioned, no specific details are listed. These details will be identified later in the main body of the course of study.

Besides stating the scope of the work to be covered, the statement should mention something concerning the emphasis which is to be placed on the mastery of skills. Thus, for a course in industrial arts, the statement needs to show that mastery of skill is not nearly as important as for a trade course where a high degree of skill is a primary requisite.

The second portion of the introductory statement should indicate the nature of the knowledge and understanding that is to be included in the course. It is not necessary at this point to actually identify each information topic. A statement specifying the broad character of the material is sufficient. A study of the examples shown at the end of the chapter will help clarify this point.

The third part of the statement should make some reference to the acquisition of desirable habits of behavior. Since the development of such qualities as working co-operatively, dependability, planning constructively, and other similar behavior characteristics, are an essential part of instruction, mention should be made in the introduction that their value will be fully recognized and activities provided for their attainment.

COURSE CONSTRUCTION

Example No. 1—Industrial Arts Woodwork

INTRODUCTORY STATEMENT

I

This course in woodwork is to give the student an opportunity to:

1. Secure broad basic experiences in the fundamentals of hand woodworking tools and woodworking processes.

2. Acquire an understanding of woods and materials used in fabricating wooden products, and the contributions made by the woodworking industry to our industrial world.

3. Develop planning and problem solving abilities and the necessary work habits and attitudes so he may adjust more readily to a changing society.

II

This industrial arts woodworking course is to cover a period of twenty weeks and is intended for eighth-grade students. Instruction is scheduled for fifty minutes, five days per week.

Example No. 2—Auto Mechanics Trade Course—First Semester

INTRODUCTORY STATEMENT

I

The first course in auto mechanics is designed to give students an opportunity to:

1. Develop the necessary skills to service and repair the running gear and power transmission system of modern automobiles.

2. Acquire the essential information concerning these phases of automotive work so they will be able to exercise good judgment in carrying out necessary repair and service operations.

3. Develop proper work habits and attitudes to enable them to maintain their jobs and live successfully in a community.

II

This course is intended for students who plan to make auto mechanics their occupation. The course is two years (four semesters) in length and is opened to students having completed the tenth grade. The class meets three consecutive hours a day for fifteen hours per week.

Fig. 2. Examples of Introductory Statements

Example No. 3—Industrial Arts General Shop

INTRODUCTORY STATEMENT

I

The industrial arts general shop course is planned to give students an opportunity to:

1. Acquire a basic understanding of the tools, materials, and processes in such areas as woods, metals, electricity, arts and crafts.

2. Acquire a knowledge of the various types of materials used in these areas and an understanding of labor and industrial management.

3. Develop desirable habits and attitudes to enable them to live as productive, co-operative, and intellectual citizens.

II

This course of study covers the activities of one semester and is designed for seventh, eighth, and ninth-grade students. The class meets for a ninety-minute period, three days per week.

Example No. 4—Machine Shop—All-Day Trade—Two Years (First Semester)

INTRODUCTORY STATEMENT

I

This course is intended to give students an opportunity to:

1. Operate safely and correctly such machines as lathe, milling machine, shaper, drill press, and grinder.

2. Acquire such knowledge as selection of suitable materials for the job, blueprint reading, shop calculations, workmen's compensation, social security regulations, and labor organizations.

3. Develop an appreciation for good craftsmanship, safety, and correct work habits.

II

This machine shop course is intended for students who are interested in seeking employment in the machine shop field. Students must have completed the tenth grade and have reached the age of sixteen years to be eligible for admission. The class meets three hours a day for a total of fifteen hours per week.

Fig. 3. Examples of Introductory Statements

Example No. 5—Animal Husbandry

INTRODUCTORY STATEMENT

I

The course in "Animal Husbandry" is intended primarily to help students:

1. Acquire the necessary skills in raising, feeding, and managing various farm animals.

2. Study the consumption characteristics, marketing system, and producer and consumer price relationship.

3. Develop those attitudes which contribute to successful and happy farm living.

II

The course is one year in length and is open to boys who are sixteen years of age or over and who plan to make farming their future vocation. The class meets daily for two consecutive hours.

Example No. 6—Clothing

INTRODUCTORY STATEMENT

I

This course in clothing is designed to give students an opportunity to:

1. Develop basic skills in making simple garments, selecting fabrics, and using commercial patterns.

2. Study manufacture and sale of fabrics.

3. Form more discriminating judgment in the selection of clothes.

4. Develop ability to plan judiciously, work co-operatively, and buy wisely.

II

The course is intended for senior high school girls. It is one year in length and the class meets 90 minutes daily.

Fig. 4. Examples of Introductory Statements

The final section of the introduction should show the time element and grade level for which the course of study is planned. This last item is especially necessary because the quantity and type of instructional material to be included in the course of study will, for the most part, be governed by the time that has been allotted to teach the course and the age or grade level for which the course is intended. In addition, if there are any prerequisites for the course, these should be mentioned.

EXAMPLES OF INTRODUCTORY STATEMENTS

Several examples are presented in Figures 2, 3, and 4 to illustrate the form that may be used to prepare introductory statements. These samples purposely have been made very brief to conserve space. In many instances the writer of a course of study will need to expand his remarks in order to make his statement clear. However, care should be taken not to bury the real meaning of the purpose in lengthy descriptive phrases.

DISCUSSION QUESTIONS

1. Why should the first step in preparing a course of study consist of writing an introductory statement?
2. The introductory statement should be expressed in terms of what four conditions?
3. Why should less emphasis be placed on mastery of skill when a course is planned for practical arts than one designed for vocational areas?
4. In preparing an introductory statement, why should some mention be made of behavior attitudes?
5. Why is it important to know the grade level and age of students when preparing a course of study?

SPECIAL ASSIGNMENT

Prepare an introductory statement for a course of study which you plan to write.

ADDITIONAL READING

Bollinger, E. W., and Weaver, G. G., *Occupational Instruction* (New York: Pitman Publishing Corporation, 1945), pp. 28–31.

Douglass, Earl R., *The High School Curriculum* (New York: The Ronald Press Company, 1947), pp. 49–69.

Jackey, David F., and Barlow, Melvin L., *The Craftsman Prepares To Teach* (New York: Macmillan, 1944), chap. 1.

Leighbody, Gerald B., *Methods of Teaching Industrial Subjects* (New York: Delmar Publishers, 1946), pp. 2–7.

Reeder, Ward G., *A First Course in Education* (New York: Macmillan, 1943), pp. 244–248.

Selvidge, R. W., and Fryklund, Verne G., *Principles of Trade and Industrial Teaching* (Peoria, Ill.: Chas. A. Bennett Company, 1930), pp. 210–254.

CHAPTER 5 ————————————

Formulating a Plan of Instructional Practices

An essential phase of a course of study is a description of the practices which are to be used in teaching a particular course. These practices actually are comparable to a given set of specifications for the fabrication of any commercial product. An architect, for example, when designing a house, not only draws detailed plans for the building but also prepares instructions as to the quality and type of materials to be used, the standards of workmanship required, specific construction procedure, and so on. Such specifications are important since they serve as guides to the builder; and, perhaps even more significant, they assure completion of the house in accordance with the architect's plans.

The teacher must also take the same precautions; he must formulate a set of standards that will help bring about the attainment of desirable learning goals. The preparation of this phase of the course of study gives the teacher an opportunity to crystallize his thinking regarding the best teaching practices to use. Furthermore, he has on record a very definite statement of some of the basic policies he intends to follow in teaching the course.

A plan of instructional practices should deal with (1) the methods of teaching to be employed, (2) the type of shop or laboratory organization to be put into operation for proper student learning, and (3) the means for measuring the effectiveness of instruction.

In this chapter some of the major teaching practices which should be described in an instructional plan will be discussed. No attempt will be made to present detailed descriptions of these practices, but only to call attention to the need to have them clearly defined in the course of study. For more complete information of teaching practices, other professional education textbooks and periodicals should be consulted.

PREPARING A PLAN OF INSTRUCTIONAL PRACTICES

The first step the writer should undertake in preparing a plan of instructional practices is to list the main topical headings that will identify the essential practices to be described. A sample of a few such topic headings follows; others may be included:

1. Teaching methods
2. Instructional aids
3. Providing for individual differences
4. Student personnel organization
5. Student planning
6. Shop finances
7. Testing and grading procedures
8. Safety
9. Shop or laboratory records

Once a list is completed, the practices or policies to be observed under each of the topic headings should be carefully described. These descriptions may be prepared either in essay or outline form.

TEACHING METHODS

The teacher of industrial arts and vocational education must use a variety of teaching methods to do an effective job. Perhaps the most widely used teaching method is the demonstration.[1] Hence, it is exceedingly important for a teacher to have a thorough understanding of all the essential features which characterize a good demonstration. Many a good teacher has started to demonstrate a valuable principle or operation, but because of his failure to have all the necessary "props," the "punch" or effectiveness of the teaching was impaired.

For some types of instructional material it will be necessary to use such teaching methods as the lecture, the discussion, or possibly class reports. The nature of the lesson, as well as the interest of the students and the ends to be reached, will to a large extent determine which method should be used. Very often the best results will be achieved by means of a short lecture; at other times a class discussion will be the most appropri-

---

[1] E. E. Ericson, *Teaching the Industrial Arts* (Peoria, Ill.: Chas. A. Bennett Co., 1946), p. 45.

ate. Frequently, a combination of teaching methods may be advisable for some particular lesson.

In preparing this section of the plan, the teaching methods which are considered most suitable for the course should be mentioned, followed by a few brief remarks concerning the activities which can be taught by these methods.[2]

INSTRUCTIONAL AIDS

The term "Instructional Aids" is used here to mean all forms of teaching devices such as film strips, motion pictures, charts, models, mock-ups, display boards, textbooks, and various other printed material. The mistake is often made of classifying instructional aids as a teaching method. In reality this is a misnomer, because aids in themselves are employed primarily to supplement teaching methods. The showing of a film or the displaying of a mock-up is simply a medium for "putting across" a particular lesson. Thus a chart may be used during a lecture to show pictorially what is being presented orally, or a model may be utilized during a demonstration to illustrate better specific operating steps of an intricate machine.

Instructional aids are considered extremely valuable because they (1) clarify verbal explanations, (2) demonstrate principles which otherwise are often difficult to visualize, and (3) add realism and interest to learning situations.

Under the heading "Instructional Aids," the writer of a course of study should express his viewpoints concerning the extent he plans to utilize aids. There is no need at this stage to actually identify specific films, charts, etc., since such identification will come later in the main body of the course of study. For this phase of the instructional plan he should confine his remarks to such matters as:

1. Why I consider aids valuable for teaching this course
2. General types of aids to be used
3. Procedure for securing aids

PROVIDING FOR INDIVIDUAL DIFFERENCES

Most teachers are frequently confronted with the problem of how to meet appropriately the individual needs and interests of students. If teaching is to fulfill its prescribed function, provisions must be made for individual differences in students. Accordingly, it is expedient during the

---

[2] John F. Friese, *Course Making in Industrial Education* (Peoria, Ill.: Chas. A. Bennett Co., 1946), p. 130.

planning of a course of study, to establish some well-defined policies which will allow students to work on their own levels of capacity. These policies must provide sufficient leeway for the slow students and, at the same time, make it possible for the more capable students to engage in activities that are a challenge to their abilities.

In thinking through an adequate plan for meeting individual differences, some consideration, therefore, should be given to such questions as:

1. Will all students work on similar projects, problems, or jobs, or will they be given some voice in the selection?
2. What specifically can be done for the slow learner?
3. How can the work be made interesting to the unusually fast learner?
4. How should instruction be handled with a group having wide ranges of interest and ability?
5. How should students be rotated through various shop or laboratory activities?

Answers to these and other questions relating to the individual differences in students should be carefully prepared while writing out this phase of the plan.

STUDENT PERSONNEL ORGANIZATION

Perhaps in no other teaching situation is a student personnel organization more important than in industrial arts and vocational education classes. A student personnel organization permits a smoother operation and administration of a school shop, and has many educational values for the students. The teacher benefits because it allows him to delegate many time-consuming details and thereby devote more time to actual teaching. The students derive benefits, since the teacher can spend more time with them. They also have an opportunity to participate in activities that provide experiences in (1) sharing and accepting responsibilities, (2) learning the significance of dependability, and (3) developing qualities of leadership.

In shops or laboratories where a great many activities are occurring simultaneously, a student personnel organization is almost a necessity if effective instruction is to take place. Students appointed to serve as leaders or foremen can assume certain managerial functions while the teacher is busily engaged in teaching one group of students. Furthermore, such an organization insures better "shopkeeping," since the instructor does not have to rely entirely on his own efforts to keep everything orderly and clean.

When a student personnel organization is drawn up, provisions should be made to include planning committees that will have the responsibility of offering suggestions concerning the improvement of shop layout and instruction. The teacher will find that students can exercise good judgment if given an opportunity to do so. They will advance many ideas to strengthen and improve the educational environment. A well-balanced and efficient student personnel plan should also include specific duties to be assigned to a shop superintendent, tool foreman, safety foreman, clean-up foreman, etc. Finally, there should be a scheme to rotate these responsibilities so all students may participate during the semester.

The preparation of this section of the course of study, therefore, should include a description of the type of student organization to be used, the procedures for administering the organization, and the nature of the responsibilities to be delegated.

STUDENT PLANNING

One of the most important aspects of any teaching situation is provision for students to plan many of their work activities. Too often teachers ignore this valuable phase of learning, even though it constitutes one of the essential objectives of industrial arts and vocational education. Learning in its broadest sense implies more than mere acquisition of knowledge and mastery of skills. In addition, there must be a development of personal qualities which will enable individuals to live more successfully well-balanced lives. Sometimes setting up experiences that lead to the attainment of specific personal attributes may seem difficult. However, this is often due to an attitude of indifference on the part of the teacher rather than the impossibility of finding suitable experiences that promote the development of these human factors. Teachers often become so imbued with their subject-matter field that they fail to devote sufficient attention to these vital personal characteristics.

It is not uncommon in many teaching situations to find all work procedures carefully planned for the students. The teacher prepares drawings of the projects, writes out detailed instructions for making them, and then personally evaluates all the finished work. A teaching organization of this kind completely overlooks a very important quality for successful living—ability to plan wisely, execute a plan, and appraise results. It would seem wise if more emphasis could be placed on the development of this one important characteristic, since it is often of greater value to students than the mastery of subject-matter content.

In addition to provisions for individual planning, there must be opportunities for group planning. Students like to work together on certain undertakings. There is no better medium for teaching co-operation than the project that requires co-operative effort. Moreover, class projects or small group projects permit use of the group for the improvement of each class member. Through deliberation and co-operative planning, students keep their own enthusiasm high, and continually give themselves direction and redirection. The teacher's influence in this is important, but teacher domination is a common weakness. The teaching procedure could be strengthened greatly if more guidance and less direction were given by the teacher. For example, students might plan to do something which would cause a serious situation. A careful teacher would avoid such planning by simply warning of the consequences and suggesting several alternatives, not by dictating another course to follow. In cases where there is just one correct way to do a given operation, the students expect the teacher to know this and to advise them of it. Their respect for him as an authority is very important, but their own planning is invaluable in attaining the broader goals of the course of study. Clear statements of policy and practice concerning student planning, therefore, should be considered an important phase of the course of study.

SHOP FINANCES

The nature of many industrial arts and vocational shops or laboratories requires that a student pay for all or part of the material used. The instructor must, therefore, set up some record system to keep an accurate account of the things used by the students. However, the teacher should refrain from personally handling any of the money; neither should this detail be delegated to any student. It is much better to have the money paid directly to the finance office or to the individual designated by the school authorities to handle school funds. Such a procedure will not only eliminate a time-consuming task, but will relieve the teacher of any possibility for personal criticism.

Accordingly, in writing up a description of instructional practices, the teacher should state specifically how he plans to handle all problems concerning shop financing.

TESTING AND GRADING

One important responsibility of a teacher is to evaluate the work of students. Many factors are involved in the grading of shop or laboratory work, and it necessitates many evaluative procedures and appraisal techniques. The teacher should first ask himself certain questions. Next, he should attempt to answer them, and, in so doing, arrive at a method for determining a student's grade.

The key question is "What factors are involved in appraising a student's performance?" This leads to the consideration of the following questions: Are work habits important? Should tardiness and absences be considered? Does the student's practice of safety for himself and others make a difference in the total evaluation? Is his performance in sharing routine maintenance duties a factor in grading? Does he accept group responsibilities? Is he a good leader? Is he a good follower? Does he plan his work well before starting it? Is he able to follow his own plans? Does he follow the plans of others better than his own? What tests of workmanship should be applied to each job, operation, or project? Should acceptable tolerances and measures vary from pupil to pupil, age level to age level, and class to class? Should the teacher award grades based on as much objective data as possible or should the grade be largely subjective in nature? Should written assignments be made? If so, what are the standards for acceptable to excellent work? Should written tests be given? If so, what type? How long? Should outside work be assigned? If so, what is its nature and how much should be expected? Furthermore, in arriving at a monthly or final grade, how much consideration should be given to the value of tests as compared to regular work assignments?

Another factor in grading is the student's evaluation of his own performance. Many teachers are coming to use students in the evaluative procedure, especially in cases where the tolerances and standards are quite well known and objective in nature.

Grades express levels of performance. Too often a teacher's philosophy results in making the spread of grades too narrow. This may cause him to show many failures, a few in-between students, and quite a few exceptional students. In actual average situations, almost the opposite is true. This does not mean, however, that all classes should represent an average of our population.

From this brief discussion of testing and grading, it does seem logical for a teacher to have a well-established plan if students are to be appraised fairly. Such a plan should be included in a course of study.

SAFETY IN THE SHOP

There is probably no other problem which is of more increasing concern everywhere than safety—safety in the home, on the highway, in industry, and school. In the final analysis, safety involves correct human behavior. If young people can be prevailed upon to develop proper attitudes of behavior, safety usually will be evident in all their endeavors.

The industrial arts and vocational education teacher undoubtedly can exert more influence in having students become safety-conscious than anyone else. The very nature of the school shop and laboratory environment, with all its physical equipment, is conducive to fostering safe habits of work. The teacher, therefore, should take full advantage of his position and regard safety as one of the most important aspects of his teaching

Safety in the school has many ramifications. There is the matter of safeguarding all hazardous equipment, arranging student work stations to prevent any form of accident, keeping the shop clean, using color dynamics, having students wear proper clothes, goggles, etc., teaching safety whenever and wherever it is necessary, and forcing students to apply safety practices in their work. In writing of safety Diamond[3] says "Many of the accidents that occur in school shops happen because someone lacked consideration for the welfare of others." Diamond states further that "If the possibility for accidents is to be reduced, pupils must be made to feel that certain safety rules must be learned and applied. It must become an obsession with them that they have a direct responsibility for their own safety as well as that of their fellow pupils. Safety practice must be in their minds constantly. The instructor must emphasize this frequently by suggesting certain rules to which everyone in the shop must conform."

If safety in the shop or laboratory is to be effective, the teacher must have a well-conceived program of safety. It seems wise, therefore, when preparing a statement of instructional practices for a course of study, to include an outline of policies governing the teaching of safety.

SHOP AND LABORATORY RECORDS

No school shop or laboratory can be run successfully without maintaining a series of records. In general, most teachers must keep an accurate and running account of these items:

1. Attendance
2. Test results
3. Inventory of equipment, tools
4. Progress of work completed by students
5. Shop finances
6. Student grades

[3] Thomas Diamond, "Safety in the School Shop," *School Shop*, April, 1952, p. 6.

When preparing a plan of instructional practices, the teacher should describe and illustrate the various forms he plans to use.

EXAMPLE OF A PLAN OF INSTRUCTIONAL PRACTICES

The following sample plan includes only a few instructional practices. The teacher, in preparing this section of the course of study, should make it as comprehensive as possible.

SECTION III

Plan of Instructional Practices

Introduction

In teaching this course in elementary woodwork, certain practices will be followed. These practices are listed herewith to insure the most effective type of instruction. From time to time some of the practices mentioned may be altered slightly to meet changes in teaching situations.

Teaching Method

To achieve the desired objectives of this course, the following teaching methods will be used.

Teaching Methods	General Classification of Activities
1. Demonstration........	Manipulative operations
2. Class discussion.....	⎰Related information ⎱Report of field trips ⎰Class organization problems
3. Shop talk............	⎰Related information ⎱Safety ⎰Motivation
4. Individual reports...	Special student assignments

Instructional Aids

Inasmuch as aids are extremely important for good teaching, every effort will be made to use as many aids as possible. Many of these aids, such as mock-

ups, models, and charts will be made in the shop.
Free literature having specific application to the
course will be obtained. Arrangements will be made
to secure worthwhile slides and motion film. In
general, the following types of aids will be used:

1. Textbooks
2. Charts, prints, posters
3. Strip films and slides
4. Motion pictures
5. Models and mock-ups

Providing for Individual Differences

To meet varying abilities in students, the following practices will be used:

1. Students will be permitted to select their own
   projects under teacher guidance.
2. Unusually capable students will be encouraged
   to work on special projects.
3. Each student will be permitted to progress at
   his own natural learning rate.
4. Special attention will be given to the slow
   learner.
5. Written reports, investigations, and other
   activities will be assigned on the basis of
   individual ability.

Student Personnel Organization

A student personnel organization will be in operation at all times. The organization will consist of
the following: superintendent, stock foreman, tool
foreman, safety engineer, and clean-up foreman.
Students elected for these duties will hold office
for a two-week period. After that, other students
will be given these assignments. A visual rotation
plan will be used so all students will have an opportunity to assume these responsibilities. Students
will wear appropriate badges to identify the position held. The duties of the various supervisory
jobs will be as follows:

Superintendent

1. Assist teacher in all shop administrative
   duties.

2. Supervise the work of the tool foreman, stock foreman, safety engineer, and clean-up foreman.
3. Have supervisory control of the bulletin board.
4. Meet shop visitors and direct them to the teacher.

Stock Foreman

1. Issue all supplies.
2. Keep stock room in order.
3. Help prepare stock for distribution.

Tool Foreman

1. Issue tools.
2. Keep tool boards in good order.
3. Repair damaged tools.
4. Report any missing tools.
5. Keep tools clean.

Clean-up Foreman

1. Assign clean-up jobs to individual students.
2. Check at the end of work period for completion of all clean-up jobs.

Safety Engineer

1. Oil machinery at designated periods.
2. Check regularly all safety devices on machines.
3. Remove objects from work areas which may be hazardous.
4. Post safety posters.

Student Planning

Students will be taught how to plan their projects, prepare their work procedure, and estimate the amount and cost of stock used. Regular student planning sheets will be provided for this purpose. In addition to individual planning, arrangements will be made for students to plan and construct some special group project.

A student-planning committee also will be appointed. The function of this committee will be to make any suggestions it considers advisable for the improvement of shop instruction.

Testing

A series of tests will be administered during the semester for the purpose of improving instruction and evaluating the progress of students. There will be a minimum of four paper tests, three of which will be of the objective type and one an essay type.

Grading

To arrive at an equitable grade, several factors will be taken into consideration. Each of these factors will be assigned a value as shown.

1. Projects.....................................50%
2. Paper tests..................................20%
3. Final examination............................10%
4. Personal growth..............................20%

DISCUSSION QUESTIONS

1. Why is a plan of instructional practices a necessary part of a course of study?
2. What are some of the essential factors that should be included in a plan of instructional practices?
3. How may students contribute greatly to evolving a plan of instruction?
4. Granted that there are many valuable learning experiences which will be left out of the course of study, how may one decide on their elimination?
5. What are some of the methods used in teaching an information and skill lesson?
6. Should many teaching methods be suggested in the course of study? Why?
7. Why should instructional aids be used? How do they supplement a particular teaching method?
8. How may guidance take precedence over direction in the planning procedure? Should it? Why?
9. What means can the teacher use to provide for individual differences?
10. What is meant by a student personnel organization? Of what value is it in a teaching situation?
11. Explain the difference between reliability and validity of measuring instruments used to establish grades.
12. Why is student planning an important element in good teaching?
13. What are some of the important factors in grading a student?
14. What precautions must be exercised in handling shop finances?

15. As a shop or laboratory teacher, what are some of the safety practices you would include in your teaching plan?
16. Describe some of the record forms you should keep.

SPECIAL ASSIGNMENT

Prepare a detailed plan of instructional practices for your particular course of study.

ADDITIONAL READING

Burns, Clyde E., "Individual Testing in the General Shop," *Industrial Arts and Vocational Education*, February, 1951, p. 64.

Colthrap, R. J., "The Demonstration," *Industrial Arts and Vocational Education*, September, 1950, p. 274.

Diamond, Thomas, "Teaching for Understanding," *School Shop*, April, 1951, p. 5.

Diamond, Thomas, "Safety in the School Shop," *School Shop*, April, 1952, p. 6.

Fales, Roy G., "Teaching Methods for the General Shop," *School Shop*, April, 1951, p. 7.

Falgren, Leon E., "Grading Industrial Arts Courses," *Industrial Arts and Vocational Education*, February, 1950, p. 41.

Gallington, Ralph O., "Improving Shop Layouts for the Industrial Arts Program," *School Shop*, April, 1949, p. 36.

Gavlak, Frank J., "Grading the Shop Student," *Industrial Arts and Vocational Education*, June, 1946, p. 254.

Halloran, Arthur J., "Shop Organization Made Easy," *School Shop*, December, 1950, p. 13.

Leighbody, Gerald B., *Methods of Teaching Industrial Subjects* (Albany, N.Y.: Delmar, Publishers, 1946), chaps. V, VI, IX, X, XI.

Micheels, W. J., and Karnes, M. R., *Measuring Educational Achievement* (New York: McGraw-Hill, 1950).

Prakken, L. W., "Principles of Good Shop Planning," *School Shop*, April, 1949, p. 5.

Sellon, William A., "The Importance of Constructing Good Tests," *Industrial Arts and Vocational Education*, February, 1951, p. 63.

Selvidge, R. W., and Fryklund, Verne C., *Principles of Trade and Industrial Teaching* (Peoria, Ill.: Chas. A. Bennett Co., 1946), chaps. VII, XIV, XX.

Stein, Edward, "Shop Student Personnel Organization," *School Shop*, September, 1943, p. 8.

Struck, F. T., *Creative Teaching* (New York: Wiley and Sons, 1938), chaps. I, II, IX, X, XI, XIV, XV, XVII, XVIII.

Weaver, Gilbert G., and Bollinger, Elroy W., *Visual Aids, Their Construction and Use* (New York: D. Van Nostrand Co., 1949).

Wilber, Gordon O., *Industrial Arts in General Education* (Scranton, Pa.: International Textbook Co., 1948), chaps. VIII, IX, XIII, XVI.

CHAPTER 6————————

Developing a Statement of Educational Philosophy

Any educational program must have as its supporting base a sound educational philosophy. A philosophy furnishes the direction or incentive that makes possible a particular kind of education. If the philosophy is inadequately defined or narrow in scope it logically follows that the resulting educational program also will be limited. In other words, the type of education established in a community depends considerably on how well its educational philosophy has been conceived.

The usual practice is for a school system to have what might be referred to as an "over-all" type of philosophy which stipulates the nature of its total educational program. Supporting this broad philosophy will be found several other statements expressing the function of various segments of the educational program. Thus, the total educational program might conceivably consist of such phases as language arts, social studies, fine arts, industrial arts, vocational, and so on. Each of these divisions would then express a more definite philosophy to support the over-all philosophy. In turn, each instructor might have a philosophy for his particular course of instruction.

Since any course of study must be predicated on some specific philosophy, the remaining portion of this chapter will be confined to a discussion of pertinent material which the teacher needs in preparing a statement of philosophy for his particular course of study.

WHAT IS MEANT BY EDUCATIONAL PHILOSOPHY

A statement of philosophy might start off with, "I believe this about industrial education: _____." Or one could begin "I feel that industrial arts is: _____," or "Vocational education is essential in American education because: _____." A philosophy is an expression of feelings, beliefs, attitudes or impressions relative to a given experience. Thus one could ask himself, "What is my philosophy of general education?" or "What are my feelings, beliefs, attitudes or impressions in respect to general education?"

Modern educational philosophy should always be based on present-day needs. For example, one might say, "Vocational education should be provided for every secondary school pupil who has a need for it and is likely to succeed in it. It should enable the student to develop enough skills so he may enter and hold a beginning position in the vocation for which he is preparing." These positive statements of philosophy can then be supported by several specific objectives. The objectives are simply expressions which translate a stated philosophy into some purposeful action. Actually, objectives are concrete statements explaining what a given phase of education or a particular course will attempt to achieve.

PHILOSOPHY OF GENERAL EDUCATION

Perhaps no better or wider accepted goals in American education are to be found than those expressed by the Educational Policies Commission of the National Educational Association. They are as follows:

"Imperative Educational Needs of Youth"[1]
1. All youth need to develop salable skills and those understandings and attitudes that make the worker an intelligent and productive participant in economic life. To this end, most youth need supervised work experience as well as education in the skills and knowledge of their occupations.
2. All youth need to develop and maintain good health and physical fitness.
3. All youth need to understand the rights and duties of the citizen of a democratic society, and to be diligent and competent in the performance of their obligations as members of the community and citizens of the state and nation.
4. All youth need to understand the significance of the family for the individual and society and the conditions conducive to successful family life.

---

[1] The Educational Policies Commission, *Education for All American Youth* (Washington: N.E.A., 1944), p. 225.

5. All youth need to know how to purchase and use goods and services intelligently, understanding both the values received by the consumer and the economic consequences of their acts.
6. All youth need to understand the methods of science, the influence of science on human life, and the main scientific facts concerning the nature of the world and man.
7. All youth need opportunities to develop their capacities to appreciate beauty in literature, art, music, and nature.
8. All youth need to be able to use their leisure time well and to budget it wisely, balancing activities that yield satisfaction to the individual with those that are socially useful.
9. All youth need to develop respect for other persons, to grow in their insight into ethical values and principles, and to be able to live and work co-operatively with others.
10. All youth need to grow in their ability to think rationally, to express their thoughts clearly, and to read and listen with understanding.

Many have concurred that all general education should tend to prepare one for present-day as well as future living. This is the pragmatist's point of view. In other words, education is life as well as a preparation for life. Perhaps the idealist would say that education is life, whereas the realist would say that education is preparation for life. With the growth of the pragmatist's philosophy in education, the vocational objective in education cannot be overlooked. General education, however, does not cover the learning provided for specific occupations. Rather, it does deal with occupational problems prevalent to many if not all vocations and contributes in some way toward the problems of earning a comfortable living and making a home.

PHILOSOPHY OF INDUSTRIAL ARTS

After the turn of the century, and especially after World War I, two very significant and revolutionary changes began to take place. These two changes were widely separated as to relationship, but each contributed greatly in the evolution of industrial arts in our public schools. The first was a change in educational *method* and the second was a change in our national *economy*. Each had a great deal to do with changes in the psychological and cultural aspects of our society.

The change in educational method began with experimentations in education based on the interests, aptitudes, and capacities of pupils. The older method was one based on the theory that transfer of training was inherent in learning, therefore mental discipline, drill and graded exercises were emphasized. Little thought was given to individual differences and needs. The new concept is to consider the learner and analyze his makeup before determining the method. Earlier, each student had the same method applied regardless of his personal peculiarities.

There was also an economic change influenced by the transition from an agrarian to an industrial nation. Whereas the older society was one in which the family was an independent unit, the present-day family is quite dependent upon the specialization of industry. Each individual has become a consumer of a multiplicity of industrial products. The development of technology has had much to do with the nature of industrial arts offerings.

Since the scope of the program of industrial arts is increasing and the problem of individual interests, aptitudes, and capacities is constantly with us, the subject matter should cut through all strata of education and extend into adult education. The content of the program is continually being expanded by both the increased interests of all age levels and the ever-increasing technological advances of industry.

Industrial arts is a part of general education which should be afforded by our public schools to all youth. It is not designed for specific occupational preparation, but for the exploration of industrial knowledge, industrial methods, hobby interests, and the development of such attitudes as will enable youth of all ages, and adults as well, to adjust more adequately to the duties and responsibilities of a democratic society dominated by the works and products of industry. More specifically, industrial arts in education is a body of selected basic learning experiences involving significant industrial activities and understandings inherent in industrial occupations, arts, and crafts of past and present civilizations, giving interpretations to: (1) the sources, refining, and distribution of raw materials used in industry, (2) the processes involved in the manufacture of industrial products, and (3) the pertinent related technical and occupational information, including group and individual safety.

A modern and purposeful industrial arts program offers opportunities for many experiences. The bulletin "Industrial Arts—Its Interpretation in American Schools"[2] states that an industrial arts program should provide for:

1. Activities in as many industries as school shops and laboratories will permit.
2. Use of typical and important industrial tools.
3. Experience in production methods.
4. Experience in handicrafts.

[2] Industrial Arts—Its Interpretation in American Schools, U.S. Office of Education, Bulletin No. 34, 1949, p. 9.

5. Acquaintance with the organization and operation of industrial and commercial enterprises.
6. Study of safe and hygienic ways of doing all types of work.
7. Practice in identifying the more important methods employed by industry.
8. Selection and use of some of the common products of industry.
9. Interpretation of the sources, principles, and applications of power, such as steam, water, internal combustion, and electricity.
10. Study of the origins and effects of significant inventions.
11. Study of materials from source to completed objects.
12. Study of vocational opportunities, living conditions, remuneration of workers, controversial questions pertaining to capital, labor, and technology.

It will be noted that these statements of industrial arts philosophy express a belief not opposed in any way to the philosophy propounded by the Educational Policies Commission for general education. In fact, this philosophy implements the basic philosophy for general education without duplicating general ideas. Industrial arts simply helps achieve the goals of general education by more specific means, making use of the subject matter it represents. Certainly more "salable skills" are represented in industrial arts than in many other subject-matter fields. Working with numerous materials and using many processes, the student of industrial arts becomes more intelligent as a productive participant in economic life. His supervised work experience is inherent in industrial arts, although his work experience may not gain him returns contained in a pay envelope. Industrial arts lays little claim to fulfilling "health" needs and "physical fitness" needs except in safety and first aid practices, but it should not hinder in any way the over-all school program. The "rights and duties of a citizen" are taught and practiced in the industrial arts class. Students share the obligations and become competent in the performance of them for the benefit of all members of the class and future classes. In industrial arts the student is given experience in the home, mechanics, home maintenance, creative design, and handicrafts, all of which contribute greatly toward "successful family life."

Through consumer education, an understanding of the values received by the consumer and the economic consequences of their acts is given great emphasis in industrial arts. Many of the methods of science and the main scientific facts concerning the nature of the world and of man are best illustrated in the materials, processes, and technology of modern industry. Industrial arts seeks to present these methods and facts as they are evolved, showing the growth of civilization from the crafts of past and present civilizations. Industrial arts gives considerable significance to experiences in creative design and construction. Through handicraft experiences youth are able to develop hoppy interests and skills which may lead to a more wholesome use of their leisure time. Shop organization and management in industrial arts provide leadership experiences, developing within students a respect for other persons and giving them an insight into ethical values and principles, thus providing for a real life situation of living and working co-operatively with others. Planning, both individual and group, gives students in industrial arts an opportunity to think rationally, express their thoughts clearly, and to read and listen with understanding. The informal atmosphere of the industrial arts shop provides for a free exchange of ideas, plans, and criticisms. In mechanical drawing and sketching, perception is developed and logical thinking and planning is promoted.

MORE SPECIFIC INDUSTRIAL ARTS OBJECTIVES

The preceding paragraph described in general the ways in which industrial arts philosophies are contributory to the greater plan of general education. To translate some of this philosophy into more specific terms, the following objectives are listed, but it must be remembered that these are less specific than individual course objectives.

1. Provide experience in correctly performing operations involving basic industrial hand tools and common machines.
2. Acquaint the students with the various fields of industry, including the materials, products, and employment opportunities.
3. Develop desirable work habits and ability to work co-operatively.
4. Develop safety habits with industrial hand tools and common machines.
5. Stimulate an interest in hobbies.
6. Develop an appreciation of good craftsmanship.
7. Provide opportunities to satisfy creative desires.
8. Develop the ability to think rationally, to plan shopwork wisely, execute plans effectively, and appraise finished products intelligently.
9. Develop the ability to select and use wisely the products of industry.
10. Develop ability to perform common household repairs.
11. Develop a basic understanding of labor-management-consumer relationships in an industrial society.

PHILOSOPHY OF VOCATIONAL EDUCATION

Vocational education presupposes that the student is beyond the exploratory stage and that his special interests are from the occupational standpoint only. Such education is a special-interest education designed for occupational preparation, involving the development of attitudes, understandings, and skills which will enable the student to adjust more adequately to the duties and responsibilities of an ethical citizen and worker in his chosen field. This special-interest education is one in which the student gets most of the basic general education needed to cope with real life situations, as well as the specific vocational training required for entry into an occupation. It is a type of education that teaches an individual to work and to perform a useful service in the society of which he is a member. Struck[3] maintains that: "Americans hold the conviction that man achieves his fullest self-realization and renders his greatest service through socially useful, efficient work. Through work, family life is stabilized; the welfare of the individual as well as of the state is advanced; and national and hemispherical security is materially strengthened."

The training of skilled workers has all too frequently been left up to the employer, especially so in the areas where new industries are being developed. The establishment of new industries and the conclusion of old ones makes for a continuous training program of vocational education in public schools a necessity. According to the first "imperative need" quoted earlier, "All youth need to develop salable skills and those understandings and attitudes that make the worker an intelligent and productive participant in economic life." Certainly it follows that a fairly large percentage of those in our public schools are likely to become employed later as craftsmen, farmers, foremen, and kindred workers.

In considering the philosophical aspects of vocational education, two significant facts are eminent. First, man has to work if he is to be associated with our form of society. By means of this work he is able to provide for his needs and comfort. How effectively he can supply his worldly necessities depends considerably on how well he has been trained to do the job for which he is best suited. It is through vocational education that he prepares himself for his job. Secondly, the perpetuation of society hinges on man's ability to render useful services.

Whenever an individual is unable to perform some service, he be-

---

[3] F. T. Struck, *Vocational Education for a Changing World* (New York: John Wiley & Sons, Inc., 1945), p. 1.

comes a liability to society. Moreover, technological leadership, which is so essential for security and continuance of the American standards of living, rests to a large extent on how well its citizenry can be trained to perform useful work. Vocational education is the medium that safeguards both human and natural resources.

Vocational education actually is not considered a part of general education, nevertheless it is a vital phase of the total educational program for the complete development of youth. Whereas general education is primarily concerned with those activities and experiences essential for successful living, vocational education deals specifically with occupational preparation. However, it is not to be presumed that vocational education is confined entirely to mastery of skills and technical knowledge. The nature of society today requires individuals who possess, in addition, comprehensive understandings of social, civic, and ethical responsibilities. Certainly the worker must be able to do the job for which he is trained, but he must also appreciate his obligations to his community and his fellow workers.

It is a well-established fact that most people lose their jobs not because they lack the technical experience but more because they fail to understand how to get along with the people with whom they work. The bulletin *Vocational Education for American Youth*[4] clearly indicates the real significance of vocational education in the following statement:

"Some years ago the term 'vocational education' was misinterpreted to mean only those forms of education or training absolutely essential for the performance of specialized occupational skills. Now, in the usually accepted sense, vocational education on the secondary level includes any and all knowledge and training that will contribute to a satisfying and useful life of employment. This involves education in general, together with emphasis on preparation for entry into an occupational field. It also includes education and training for those employed persons who need further knowledge or added skills to keep pace with changing conditions and to retain employment already held. It may provide training for improvement or advancement in such employment, or for transfer from one field of occupation to another as made necessary by technological changes."

It is sometimes implied that vocational education commences upon the termination of the general education program. A course of instruc-

---

[4] *Vocational Education for American Youth* (Washington, D.C.: American Vocational Association, 1949), p. 3.

tion based on this premise is doomed to failure according to modern educational practices. Vocational education should begin when the individual is ready for employment, but running concurrently with such a program there needs to be a functional "strand" of general education.

In order that there be no misunderstanding as to the criteria for the content of vocational education, six measures are presented as follows:

1. There should be student skills developed in all typical and basic processes inherent in the occupations involved.
2. There should be pupil experiences in the interpretation and use of fundamental factual information basic to the occupation.
3. There should be experiences in related science, mathematics, mechanical drawing, and other tool subjects related to the occupation.
4. There should be learning experiences provided for the pupil whereby he learns all about the hazards, benefits, joys, and sorrows connected with his chosen occupation.
5. There should be learning experiences provided for the pupil whereby he is enabled to see his prospective occupation in relationship to management, labor, and the professions.
6. There should be learning experiences in general education which will enable the student to take his place in life and fulfill his life's needs as an enlightened citizen and worker.

MORE SPECIFIC VOCATIONAL OBJECTIVES

The following might be considered as representing more specific objectives in support of a vocational philosophy.

1. Develop specific skills and related knowledge associated with the occupation involved.
2. Develop an understanding of labor and management.
3. Develop pride in work and an appreciation for craftsmanship.
4. Develop occupational safety habits and understandings.
5. Develop ability to co-operate with fellow workers in the occupation involved.
6. Develop individual initiative and responsibilities as a worker.
7. Develop ability to solve problems.
8. Stimulate the development of leadership qualities.
9. Foster the development of self-reliance.

PREPARING A STATEMENT OF EDUCATION PHILOSOPHY

Section IV of the course of study should consist of three parts. First, there should be a statement of the "over-all philosophy" adopted by the school system for the education of its youth. Second, there should be a brief explanation of the philosophy of the specific field for which the course of study is being prepared. Third, there should be a list of objectives to support the stated philosophy of the special subject field. It is not necessary in this section to mention specific course objectives. These will be discussed in Chapter VII. A sample of how Section IV may be prepared follows:

SECTION IV
Statement of Educational Philosophy

I. Educational Philosophy for School System

The primary function of the educational program in the public school system of Kingstown is:

1. Self-Realization:

   To develop the following traits in the student: an inquiring mind, good speech, good reading habits, good writing, mathematics, observation, knowledge of health (personal and public), recreation, esthetic interests, and personal character.

2. Human Relationships:

   To develop respect for humanity, personal friendships, co-operation, courtesy, appreciation for home life, and developing democracy and homemaking.

3. Economic Efficiency:

   Development and appreciation and knowledge of: work, occupational requirements, occupational choice, occupational efficiency, occupational adjustment, occupational appreciation, personal economics, consumer judgment, buying efficiency, and consumer protection.

4. Civic Responsibility:

   To bring understanding of: social practices, social activity, judgment, insight, tolerance, conservation of resources, social application of science, world citizenship responsibilities, observance of law, understanding of economics, political responsibility, and devotion to country.

II. Basic Philosophy of Industrial Arts

Industrial Arts is an essential phase of a modern program of general education for all people. It provides experiences in the use of materials, tools, and equipment and a knowledge of the processes and products of industry and their social and economic significance to the life of the community and the nation.

This is an industrial age; modern living requires that all citizens have a more adequate understanding of industrial processes and problems. Technological changes affect the economic and social status of all people. Invention and science have changed whole industries and replaced others. Mass production has provided thousands of industrial occupations for those who formerly worked on farms or in allied occupations. Many now make a living by industrial production alone or in connection with part-time farming. These developments call for much more manipulative and technical training and experience on the part of every person for an understanding of the age in which we live, and a valuable foundation for the thousands who will make their livelihood in industrial or allied occupations.[5]

III. Objectives of Industrial Arts[6]

1. Citizenship
   To provide an opportunity for individual development of desirable attitudes, characteristics, interests and habits through participation in an interesting activity program.
2. Craftsmanship
   To provide for learning to plan and construct things of value and beauty involving the use of the more common hand tools and machines.
3. Cultural
   To provide an opportunity for students to develop a more realistic appreciation of

---

[5] Michigan Industrial Education Society, Industrial Arts in Michigan, 1946.
[6] Ibid.

the beauty and value of products of the
world in which we live.
4. Consumer Knowledge
   To develop the ability to select and use
   intelligently the materials and products
   of industry.
5. Worthy Home Membership
   To provide an opportunity for students to
   become familiar with, and interested in,
   maintenance and improvements in the home.
6. Guidance and Exploration
   To help each student to determine whether
   or not he has special aptitudes of a manipulative nature and the necessary information
   to consider and plan further educational
   experiences.
7. Avocational
   To provide exploratory experiences in
   several of the more common leisure-time
   activities in which people engage.
8. Occupational
   To provide experiences in a well-rounded
   educational program which provide founda-
   tions for living and working in an industrial community.

DISCUSSION QUESTIONS

1. What is the difference between a philosophy and an objective?
2. What are some of the characteristics of shop layout which would indicate a teacher's philosophy?
3. Why should objectives be included in a course of study?
4. What skills are teachers supposed to have in order to attain objectives?
5. What is the nature of general education? Who is it for? How is it different from industrial arts education?
6. What vocational objectives has industrial arts?
7. What vocational objectives has general education?
8. How are the objectives of vocational education different from those of general education? Industrial arts?
9. What are some conflicting philosophies observed in schools or communities with which you are familiar?
10. Which should evolve first, philosophy or objectives?

SPECIAL ASSIGNMENT

Prepare a statement of philosophy and supporting objectives for the course of study which you are preparing.

ADDITIONAL READING

Ashley, Lloyd W., "Two Sides of the Coin," *School Shop*, December, 1948, p. 5.

Friese, John F., *Course Making in Industrial Education* (Peoria, Ill.: Chas. A. Bennett Co., 1946), pp. 58–67.

Hardin, Robert A., "Our Evolving Philosophy of Industrial Arts," *Industrial Arts and Vocational Education*, May, 1950, p. 179.

Harris, F. H., "Objectives of Industrial Education," *Industrial Arts and Vocational Education*, January, 1950, p. 7.

Kissinger, Herbert, "Democracy in School Shop," *School Shop*, December, 1949, p. 7.

Lamb, Auburn J., "This I Do Believe," *School Shop*, January, 1951, p. 7.

London, H. H., "Background and Outlook in Industrial Education," *Industrial Arts and Vocational Education*, September, 1949, p. 257.

Mays, Arthur B., "The Concept of Vocational Education in the Thinking of the General Educator, 1845 to 1945" (Urbana, Ill.: University of Illinois, 1946), Bulletin No. 65, p. 107.

McCarthy, John A., *Vocational Education: America's Greatest Resource* (Chicago: American Technical Society, 1950), pp. 148–210, 291–324.

Pawelek, Stanley, "Two Phases of Our Field," *School Shop*, May, 1944, p. 10.

Proffitt, Maris M., "How Goes Industrial Arts," *School Shop*, October, 1941, p. 3.

Reeder, Ward, *A First Course in Education* (New York: Macmillan), chap. II.

Shattuck, Edward A., "A Curricular View of Industrial Education," *Industrial Arts and Vocational Education*, April, 1950, p. 147.

Struck, F. Theodore, *Vocational Education for a Changing World* (New York: Wiley, 1945), pp. 1–83.

Stucki, Ralph E., "Modern Industrial Arts," *Industrial Arts and Vocational Education*, September, 1950, p. 258.

Vocational Education for American Youth, American Vocational Association, Washington, D.C., 1949, p. 11.

Wilber, Gordon O., *Industrial Arts in General Education* (Scranton, Pa.: International Textbook Company, 1948), p. 32.

Willoughby, George, "Objectives in Industrial Arts," *School Shop*, September, 1948, p. 22.

CHAPTER 7

Establishing Specific Course Objectives

The advisability of identifying a definite philosophy and its supporting aims or objectives when preparing a course of study was discussed in the last chapter. The purpose of this chapter is twofold—first, to indicate the need of establishing specific course objectives, and second, to show the importance of analyzing the course objectives in terms of the activities that may be provided to actually achieve the selected objectives.

MISCONCEPTION OF OBJECTIVES

Most courses of study usually contain a long list of objectives, but rarely is any evidence shown as to how these objectives can be fulfilled. The supposition seems to be that by merely cataloging the objectives, their implementation is assured and nothing further needs to be done. Unfortunately, this is wishful thinking because no single objective can be expected to materialize unless definite provisions are made for its attainment. Wilber[1] expresses this viewpoint when he says: "It is not sufficient to subscribe to a set of aims and then forget about them, or to keep them in the desk drawer to be shown to those who may be interested. Rather, these objectives must become the foundation and bulwark of the whole program. Before this is possible, however, one must analyze them carefully in terms of the outcomes expected."

Most teachers of industrial arts and vocational education will agree that educational objectives are important and essential guides for effec-

---

[1] Gordon O. Wilber, *Industrial Arts in General Education* (Scranton, Pa.: International Textbook Co., 1948), p. 45.

tive instruction. Yet it is questionable if sufficient thought is ever given to objectives to insure an understanding of their implications. Far too many teachers simply accept objectives as necessary platitudes or ornamental generalities to be displayed and admired. This point of view is substantiated by Krug[2] who writes: "Too many elaborate statements of objectives have been fought over, refined and super-refined, and then relegated to the files while the school goes merrily on without discernible change." Friese[3] maintains that: "Frequently aims have been set up which were very idealistic or philosophical, so much so that their achievement was impossible because of inadequate contributing subject matter or method."

The writers of most courses of study will usually spend a great deal of time analyzing a course for its basic operations, related information, and projects. Rarely is comparable consideration given to the activities which are needed to make worth-while objectives function in a teaching situation. Take, for example, such an objective as "teaching pupils to work co-operatively." All will agree that the achievement of this goal is highly desirable. But students cannot be taught to work co-operatively unless certain activities are established in the instructional program to give them experience in working together. It is true that the attainment of some goals is often difficult to measure. Nevertheless, as much thought should be given to the achievement of objectives as to other instructional phases of the course.

SELECTING SPECIFIC COURSE OBJECTIVES

At this point in the preparation of a course of study, the teacher should carefully study the broad objectives which were previously listed for general education and those for his special field. From this list he should select those objectives which he feels have a definite relationship to his course. Each objective should be analyzed from the standpoint of the activity which can be provided to promote its development, and then the objective retained or rejected on the basis of the facilities available to place the activity into operation. If, for example, the writer of a course of study is to accept the objective "to promote creative thinking" as worthy of attainment, then he must ask himself the question, "What

[2] Edward A. Krug, *Curriculum Planning* (New York: Harper & Bros., 1950), p. 5.
[3] John F. Friese, *Course Making in Industrial Education* (Peoria: Chas. A. Bennett Company, 1946), p. 80.

form of instructional experiences can I provide that will furnish practice in creative thinking?" Only by subjecting all objectives to this form of evaluation is there any assurance that they will become realistic, meaningful, and valuable instructional instruments.

CONVERTING OBJECTIVES INTO STUDENT OUTCOMES

Objectives, when compiled as such, are simply passive statements of intent; that is, descriptive phrases representing and supporting a particular educational philosophy. After objectives have been analyzed and specific activities for their attainment identified, then these objectives become operational actions and thereby might more appropriately be labeled outcomes. By designating them as outcomes, the objectives are placed in the same category of things to be taught as manipulative operations and related information. Thus, "how to plane a board square" may be considered a specific skill outcome, and the construction of book ends as the medium for acquiring this skill. Similarly, the objective "how to solve problems" might be one of the outcomes and provision for students to plan their project, the medium for attaining this outcome. In both cases the skill and the objective now represent teachable content and as a result become a definite part of the instructional program.

The most difficult aspect of transforming objectives into outcomes is determining the appropriate activities that will provide the type of experiences required. For the most part, these activities may be in the form of several experiences in one or more of the following:

1. Working on individual and group projects
2. Student personnel shop organization
3. Field trips
4. Shop planning committees
5. Student project planning
6. Student evaluation of projects
7. Interviews and visitations with labor and management
8. Providing suggestion box
9. Analyzing good and poor commercial products
10. Safety committees
11. Opportunities for Experimentation
12. Arranging for outside speakers to talk to the class

The above should be viewed only as suggestions; undoubtedly, the teacher, in preparing a course of study, will think of many others. Regardless of the type of activity chosen, it must be described in very specific terms; otherwise it becomes another meaningless generality.

EXAMPLES OF EXPECTED STUDENT OUTCOMES

It is recommended that this section of the course of study be labeled "Specific Course Objectives." A short introductory paragraph should follow explaining the purpose of this material. Then it is suggested that the expected outcomes be listed in one column, and the activities selected as a means of achieving the goals be listed opposite the outcomes. In a later chapter instructions will be given for inserting these activities in the main body of the course of study. Listed below are a few examples of outcomes and suggested types of activities.

SECTION V

Specific Course Objectives
(Woodwork)

Student Outcomes	Activities to Achieve Outcomes
1. To interpret the importance of the woodworking industry	1. Visit to several woodworking industries 2. Individuals to present reports on some phase of the woodworking industry 3. Panel discussion on the topic, "Contributions of the woodworking industry to home and family living"
2. Develop good habits of work	1. Provide specific standards for each work job. Discuss these with students 2. Provide a clean, well-organized shop that is conducive to good learning 3. Discuss with students the importance of good work habits in relation to industrial practice, job advancement, etc. 4. Measure student's work objectively 5. Provide means for students to plan their work accurately and methodically

Student Outcomes	Activities to Achieve Outcomes
3. Develop some degree of skill in using basic hand tools	1. Series of individual projects 2. Several practice exercises 3. One group project
4. Develop recreational and avocational activities	1. Make available to students such magazines as "Popular Mechanics," "Popular Science," etc. 2. Talk to students about their outside activities 3. Provide opportunities for students to work on their hobbies in the shop 4. Arrange a hobby show 5. Sponsor hobby clubs such as boat and model airplane building, photography, etc.
5. Develop ability to work co-operatively	1. Provide student personnel organization 2. Set up several class or group projects 3. Encourage students to seek help from each other 4. Provide student shop planning committees 5. Assign more advanced students to help students needing assistance
6. Understand labor and management	1. Assign reading in several trade magazines 2. Arrange for talks by men in industry representing both labor and management 3. Schedule discussions on problems dealing with: a) Labor Unions b) Responsibilities of Management c) Personnel Relations

Student Outcomes	Activities to Achieve Outcomes
	4. Provide suggestion box for ideas in running a shop
7. Develop an appreciation of good craftsmanship	1. Have students analyze products for good and poor design, construction, etc.
	2. Arrange field trips through two factories, one a producer of cheap furniture, the other a producer of good furniture
	3. Discuss principles of good design
	4. Correlate shopwork with the Art Department
	5. Provide contest to display projects of good design
8. Develop good safety habits	1. Display safety posters
	2. Provide safety devices on all machines
	3. Set up a student committee on safety
	4. Demonstrate correct safety practices whenever appropriate
	5. Show movies on safety
	6. Arrange for talks by members of Safety Council in industry
9. Develop ability to solve problems	1. Provide for students to design and plan their projects
	2. Provide a plan for students to appraise their work

DISCUSSION QUESTIONS

1. How can objectives be made more meaningful in an educational situation?
2. What are some of the misconceptions of educational objectives in terms of their achievements?

3. Is there any justification in providing means for attaining a specific objective if its achievement cannot be fully measured? Explain.
4. What factors should be considered in selecting specific objectives for a particular course?
5. What is the difference between educational objectives and student outcomes?

SPECIAL ASSIGNMENT

Select the specific objectives which you believe are attainable for your course and list the activities which you plan to provide that will furnish the necessary experiences to achieve these objectives.

ADDITIONAL READING

A guide to Improving Instruction in Industrial Arts (Washington, D.C.: American Vocational Association, 1953).

Ericson, Emanuel E., *Teaching the Industrial Arts* (Peoria, Ill.: Chas. A. Bennett Co., 1946), chap. XI.

Friese, John F., *Course Making in Industrial Education* (Peoria, Ill.: Chas. A. Bennett Co., 1946), chap. VI.

Giachino, J. W., "Am I a Good Teacher?" *School Shop*, April, 1948, p. 15.

Industrial Arts Laboratory, Chicago Board of Education, Chicago, 1953.

Kissinger, J. H., "Democracy in the School Shop," *School Shop*, December, 1949, p. 7.

Krug, Edward A., *Curriculum Planning* (New York: Harper & Bros., 1950), chap. I.

Newkirk, Louis V., and Johnson, Wm. H., *The Industrial Arts Program* (New York: The Macmillan Co., 1948), chaps. IV, V, VI.

Rathburn, Jesse E., "Fill the Vacuum," *School Shop*, June, 1951, p. 7.

Wilber, Gordon O., *Industrial Arts in General Education* (Scranton, Pa.: International Textbook Company, 1948), chap. V.

CHAPTER 8 ———————————

The Instructional Analysis

The process of selecting the course content is known as instructional analysis. The analysis is actually a technique of making an inventory of all the learning activities that are associated with a specific instructional area. This analysis not only insures complete coverage of the important teachable elements, but it also makes possible the arrangement of these elements into a logical teaching order. The analysis eliminates the hit-and-miss probability of providing a meaningful and fruitful course of instruction. It does not leave to chance or memory that which should be taught or needs to be accomplished.

FUNCTION OF THE INSTRUCTIONAL ANALYSIS

A properly organized course of study should disclose the following five principal categories of data:
1. Operations
2. Jobs, projects, or problems
3. Related information
4. Special activities
5. Instructional aids

The function of the analysis is to select the appropriate material for each of the above categories and to arrange this material into a logical teaching sequence. The method of analyzing the information for each of these groups will be discussed in the chapter to follow.

IDENTIFYING THE MAIN DIVISIONS OF A COURSE

The first step in making an instructional analysis is to determine the main divisions of the course. These divisions are frequently called blocks.[1] A division may be defined as a broad unit of instruction in which the manipulative work and informational material have closely related elements. In machine shop the divisions might be centered around different machines such as the lathe, milling machine, shaper, drill press, etc. Thus, the instructional elements in each of these divisions will have certain things in common. The lathe division will involve work that is characteristic of the lathe; the shaper division will deal with content that is peculiar to the shaper, and so on.

Very often these divisions represent distinct classifications of work, functions, industrial areas, or trades. A course of study for industrial arts general shop may have activities grouped under such divisions as woodwork, metalwork, electricity, and plastics. Welding may be divided into two blocks—oxyacetylene and electric arc. A course for automotive mechanics might logically be organized into such divisions as engine, power transmission, chassis, electrical and body repair. A course in foods might be divided into the areas of food preparation, nutrition, serving, planning, and buying. The divisions of a course in agriculture may be dairying and feeding, poultry raising, farm crops, and soils. A beauty culture course might possibly have such divisions as hair cutting and styling, hair dying or tinting, manicuring and hair dressing.

During the process of identifying the main divisions of the course, it will be advisable to assign tentatively a period of time that may be devoted to each block. This timetable will serve two purposes: (1) it will be a guide as to the amount of instructional material that is to be included in each division, and (2) it will insure proper distribution of learning experiences. Without such a time schedule it is quite possible that the greater portion of the semester may be spent on one or two divisions and the remaining blocks of instruction then minimized because of insufficient time.

To arrive at some equitable distribution of time for the various divisions, the instructor should be guided by (1) the complexity of the work that is peculiar to the division, (2) the importance of the work in relation to the over-all goals to be reached, and (3) the time available for teaching the entire course. A machine shop teacher may reason that since there are a great many more manipulative operations to be learned on a lathe than on a drill press, a greater proportion of the available time should be assigned to lathe work.

The timetable for the various blocks of the course may necessitate

[1] Verne C. Fryklund, *Trade and Job Analysis* (Milwaukee: Bruce Publishing Company, 1947), p. 73.

some modification after the analysis is completed. When a satisfactory distribution of time is reached, the information can be shown in the course of study somewhat as follows:

DIVISIONS OF THE COURSE	WEEKS
1. Lathe	5
2. Milling machine	4
3. Drill press	2
4. Shaper	3
5. Benchwork	3
6. Grinder	1

SUBDIVISIONS

Some courses cannot be broken down into major blocks as previously described. For example, it would be somewhat difficult to divide a one-semester sheetmetal or blueprint reading course into major divisions. In such cases the instructional material might be appropriately grouped into smaller units. The subdivisions in bench metalwork could be headed as follows:

1. Layout work
2. Cutting metal
3. Bending, twisting, and forming metal
4. Assembling
5. Decorating and finishing metal

In bench woodwork the subdivisions might be identified as:

1. Layout and planning
2. Cutting and shaping
3. Assembling
4. Finishing

In clothing the subdivisions might be:

1. Fundamentals of hand sewing
2. Fundamentals of machine sewing
3. Patterns, cutting, and garment construction
4. Shirring, ruffles, tucks, pleats, and hems
5. Collars and sleeves
6. Buttons and fasteners

A personality development course may have subdivisions as:

1. Appearance
2. Color

3. Appropriate attire
4. Beauty aids
5. Grooming habits

It should be remembered that these subdivisions are merely convenient means of organizing instructional material. The selection of the subdivision title headings is largely an arbitrary procedure; the instructor should use such minor divisions, as they might appear justifiable for his course. The actual identification of subdivision headings, as well as the grouping of the material under these headings, can be accomplished better after the course is analyzed for its instructional content.

DISCUSSION QUESTIONS

1. What is the principal function of an instructional analysis?
2. What is meant by divisions of a course?
3. What are some of the identifying features of a division?
4. What factors should be considered in determining the amount of material that should be included in the various divisions of a course?
5. Of what significance are subdivisions in organizing a course of study?

SPECIAL ASSIGNMENT

Think through your course and determine if it can be broken down into divisions. Identify these divisions and tentatively assign a time value to each.

ADDITIONAL READING

Bollinger, Elroy W., and Weaver, Gilbert G., *Occupational Instruction* (New York: Pitman Publishing Co., 1945), pp. 15–18.

Fryklund, Verne C., *Trade and Job Analysis* (Milwaukee, Wis.: The Bruce Publishing Co., 1947), chap. IV.

Micheels, W. J., "The Analysis Technique," *Industrial Arts and Vocational Education*, November, 1949, p. 349.

CHAPTER 9

Analyzing a Course for Its Basic Operations

One of the distinguishing characteristics of industrial arts and vocational education courses is that they provide experiences involving manipulative work. The degree of skill to be mastered in performing this type of work depends considerably on the ends to be achieved. Thus, for a class that is established strictly on a vocational level, the development of skill is far more important than for an industrial arts course. Nevertheless, the method of identifying the course content is the same for all areas.

Since the manipulative work generally serves as the main basis of a course, it seems only logical that the first consideration, when choosing the course content, is the selection of those things which make up the manipulative processes. The purpose of this chapter is to discuss the procedure for identifying the basic operations of a course.

MEANING OF OPERATIONS

Fryklund,[1] in his work on trade analysis, defines an operation as a unit of work that involves depicting, or the forming, or the shaping of material, or the assembling of parts. Bollinger and Weaver[2] describe an operation as an element of a trade which the worker does with tools, machines, and materials. They further state that every item involves ac-

---

[1] Verne C. Fryklund, *Trade and Job Analysis* (Milwaukee, Wis.: The Bruce Publishing Co., 1947), p. 42.

[2] E. W. Bollinger and G. G. Weaver, *Occupational Instruction* (New York: Pitman, 1945), pp. 12–15.

tion, and the operation is best described by means of such action verbs as bend, adjust, cut, fold, drape, mix, curl, etc.

The dictionary defines an operation as a method of exercising or applying force; a mode of action; a single specific act; an act or process of operating. It would seem, then, that an operation is a manipulative process performed while transforming an unfinished product into a finished article, or a unit of work to be executed in repairing, installing, adjusting, preparing or replacing any part of a fabricated product. The above definition implies two main types of operations. These might be appropriately called *production operations* and *servicing operations*.

PRODUCTION OPERATIONS

A production operation is performed during the process of manufacturing an article. As such, it is only one of a series of things that must be done to produce the article. An example of this would be "reaming a hole" or "cutting metal with a hacksaw." These two operations might be executed in making a lamp, a fixture, or a jig, or in constructing countless other articles. In each instance, the manner of executing the operation remains the same regardless of the shape, size, or kind of article to be fabricated. A production operation might involve making a hem, preparing buttonholes, stitching, or cutting a pattern. Except for some minor modifications, the procedure in performing these operations will not change whether the garment being made is a blouse, dress, or jacket.

It is important to note, then, that a production operation always involves the construction of some specific article.

SERVICING OPERATIONS

A servicing operation is one that is performed when it is necessary either to modify the shape of a product or to restore it into a usable condition. This operation involves adjusting, cleaning, replacing, installing, or repairing something. An illustration of a servicing operation may be the adjustment of a carburetor, the cleaning of spark plugs, the repair of a leak in a tire, the installation of a wing on an airplane, or the replacement of an electric cord in a lamp. Additional illustrations of servicing operations might be washing hair, waving hair, preparing a sales slip, feeding hogs, planting corn, washing glassware. All the above-mentioned operations are accomplished to bring about some change in a product and, unlike production operations, do not necessarily involve the construction of some specific article.

HOW TO DESIGNATE AN OPERATION

It is customary to express an operation with an introductory phrase "how to." Here are a few examples:

1. How to file metal
2. How to chamfer an edge
3. How to ink a press
4. How to solder
5. How to varnish a surface
6. How to rivet a joint
7. How to sift flour
8. How to roll out pie crust
9. How to carve fowl
10. How to apply a zipper
11. How to sew a fell seam
12. How to make hems

Sometimes the verb "how" is eliminated and only the infinitive form "to" is retained. In this manner the operation is expressed as "to twist metal" instead of "how to twist metal." Some teachers prefer to state the operation with a present participle such as "filing metal," "drilling holes," "cutting a taper," etc. The manner of designating the operation is relatively unimportant. However, consistency in the use of one form or another is desirable.

When listing operations, it is better to avoid stating them in terms of tool or machine usage such as "how to use a chisel" or "how to use a band saw." The tool or machine serves only as the implement needed to perform some part of the operation. Very often several tools may be required to perform the operation. Then again the same tool or machine may be used in one way for one operation and in another way for a different operation. Obviously, teaching an operation in this way would complicate the lesson, since it is virtually impossible to teach all the ways a tool can be used in any one lesson.[3] Moreover, it would be extremely difficult to show the complete units of work for any given instructional area if the operations were listed entirely on the basis of tools and machines used.

HOW TO IDENTIFY AN OPERATION

As mentioned previously, an operation deals either with making or servicing a product. It is quite possible for a beginning teacher to be

---

[3] Verne C. Fryklund, *Trade and Job Analysis* (Milwaukee, Wis.: The Bruce Publishing Co., 1947), pp. 42–43.

slightly confused at times as to whether an operation is actually an operation in itself, or whether it is simply a part of a basic operation. In general, its identity can be assured if the operation actually permits being demonstrated as a complete lesson. One of the characteristics of an operation is that it has a purpose of its own and provides a suitable unit of instruction. For example, suppose there is some question as to whether or not "center punching holes" is an operation. By analyzing what is to be done, it can readily be concluded that "center punching holes" does not contain enough teachable material for a suitable demonstration. Center punching holes is really a step in the performance of the main operation "drilling holes." Another example might be "how to apply soldering flux." An examination of what is involved in applying flux will disclose that a demonstration of this alone would be quite meaningless. Applying flux is only a step in the basic operation "soldering." The same would be true in "how to apply a shampoo." Applying a shampoo is not an actual operation but merely a step in the basic operation of "how to wash hair."

The element of teaching time is not necessarily a factor in identifying an operation. Some operations may be demonstrated in a comparatively short period of ten or fifteen minutes, while more complicated operations may require a thirty-minute demonstration.

Another aspect of an operation is that it requires several specific things to be done in a certain sequential order. Unless the operation can reasonably be broken down into a number of well-defined performing steps, in all probability it cannot justifiably be considered a purposeful operation. Samples of operations with their performing steps follow:

HOW TO RIVET

Performing Steps
1. Lay out locations of rivets
2. Center punch holes
3. Select correct size drill
4. Drill holes
5. Remove burrs
6. Insert and buck rivet

HOW TO MAKE AN OMELET

Performing Steps
1. Beat eggs with cream and seasonings
2. Melt butter in pan
3. Pour in egg mixture and stir slowly
4. Tilt pan slightly and draw omelet to one side of pan
5. Remove when golden brown

75

VEHICLES OF INSTRUCTION

Vehicles of instruction refer to the instructional medium which embodies the selected operations. Such vehicles may be designated as "jobs," "projects," "problems," or "activities." It is relatively unimportant by what name these vehicles are called. For some courses it may be more convenient or appropriate to label them jobs or projects. In some areas the term problem or activity may be more suitable. The method of selecting the proper instructional media will be discussed in greater detail in Chapter XI.

PROCEDURE FOR LISTING THE OPERATIONS

1. Secure a pack of 3" x 5" cards. Write down a single operation on each card. If the course has several main divisions, complete the listing of the operations for one division before going on with the next. Do not be concerned at this point about the correct order of teaching these operations. Furthermore, it is not necessary to designate them as production or servicing operations. Simply write them down. See Fig. 5.

2. When all the operations are recorded, determine whether or not

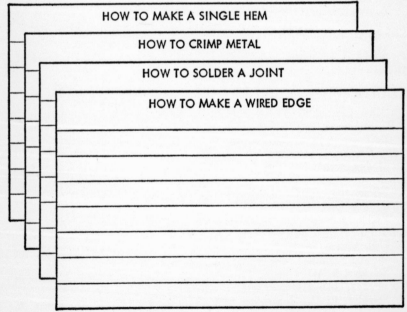

Fig. 5. Operations Listed on 3" x 5" Cards

any important operations have been omitted. This may be done by consulting other courses of study: textbooks, pamphlets, periodicals, and trade literature.

3. Once the list is completed, decide which operations are to be eliminated and those which are to be retained and taught. The amount of time that is available to teach the course and the goals to be achieved will determine what operations will be included in the course. A one-semester industrial arts course in electricity logically would contain fewer operations than a similar course established on a trade level. The instructor will have to rely on his experience and judgment in choosing the operations to be discarded.

DISCUSSION QUESTIONS

1. What is the difference between a production operation and a servicing operation?
2. How should operations be designated?
3. What is the argument against listing operations in terms of tool usage?
4. How is it possible to judge whether a unit of work is actually an operation or only a performing step?
5. How is it possible to determine whether the list of operations is complete?
6. What is meant by a job or project?

SPECIAL ASSIGNMENT

Using 3" x 5" cards, list the operations for the course of study which you are in the process of preparing.

ADDITIONAL READING

Allen, Charles R., *The Instructor, the Man and the Job* (Philadelphia: J. B. Lippincott Co., 1919), chaps. V, VI, VII, VIII.

Bollinger, E. W., and Weaver, G. G., *Occupational Instruction* (New York: Pitman, 1945), chap. II.

Dodge, Arthur F., "Jobs Versus Operations," *School Shop*, June, 1947, p. 10.

Friese, John F., *Course Making in Industrial Education* (Peoria, Ill.: Chas. A. Bennett Co., 1946), chap. VIII.

Fryklund, Verne C., *Trade and Job Analysis* (Milwaukee, Wis.: The Bruce Publishing Co., 1947), chap. IV.

Hill, Warren E., and Ewing, Claude H., *Materials and Methods for Vocational Training* (New York: McGraw-Hill Co., 1942), chap. II.

Selvidge, R. W., *How to Teach a Trade* (Peoria, Ill.: Chas. A. Bennett Co., 1923), chap. III.

Selvidge, R. W., *Individual Instruction Sheets* (Peoria, Ill.: Chas. A. Bennett Co., 1934), chaps. II, III.

CHAPTER 10

Arranging Operations in an Instructional Order

When the operations for a course have been identified, the next step is to arrange these operations into a logical teaching sequence. Two techniques may be used—the card method and the chart method. Both of these techniques will be discussed in this chapter.

BASIC CRITERIA FOR ARRANGING OPERATIONS

There are three important factors to consider in arranging operations into a good learning order. They are:

1. Early need
2. Frequency of use
3. Correct order of performance

Early need means that those operations which students must perform immediately when starting a project or job should be taught first. For example, one of the first things a student has to do to make a project in a metalworking class is to secure the correct size stock. To accomplish this he must know how to measure. The operation "How to Measure," therefore, must be considered as one of the first operations to teach.

Frequency of use means that those operations which students perform frequently, regardless of the nature of the job or project, must be taught early in the course. In the metalworking course already mentioned, filing is an operation that a student must do repeatedly on his first and successive projects. Obviously, this operation should be taught early, so students will not be hampered in carrying out their work and learning additional operations as they are needed.

Correct order of performance means that operations must be taught in a certain sequential order regardless of their difficulty. In the normal process of constructing a project, one operation must be completed before another is started. Thus, it is usually necessary to saw a board before planing it square, and to sand a surface before applying stain or shellac. If operations were arranged on the basis of difficulty, it is conceivable that one operation would need to be taught first even though its execution would be delayed until some other operation was learned. The factor of difficulty is somewhat relative because no standard can be applied to indicate that one operation is more difficult than another. What might be a complex operation for one student may be easy for another.

In general, then, any plan used to arrange operations in a proper teaching order must take into consideration, first, those operations a student will be required to do early; second, those operations that are performed frequently; and third, the natural order of executing operations.

CARD METHOD FOR SECURING AN INSTRUCTIONAL ORDER—SERVICING OPERATIONS

If the course being analyzed consists of servicing type of operations, the card method must be used to secure a proper instructional order. One of the characteristics of servicing operations is that the operations themselves constitute the jobs to be learned. Whereas special projects are used as a medium to learn productive type operations, no particular articles are needed for servicing operations. For example, "Adjusting a Carburetor" is a servicing operation and the learning medium is the experience provided in actually performing this work. The process of adjusting a carburetor is the task involved and as such it becomes a purposeful job. On the other hand, "Filing Metal" is a production operation and, if this operation is to be functional, it must be associated with some project. The mere act of filing is meaningless; it has educational value only when it is performed on some useful work.

The following procedure should be used to arrange servicing operations into an instructional order.

1. Take the 3″ x 5″ cards on which the operations were originally listed (Chapter IX) and spread them on a table or desk. Work with one division at a time.

2. Check through the cards and pick out all the operations that students must learn to do early. Arrange these cards so that each operation follows a logical order of performance.

3. Select those cards on which are listed the operations that have to be performed frequently. Again arrange these cards so the operations fall in a correct order of performance and place them below the first group of cards.

4. Arrange the remaining cards so each operation falls in the proper order of performance and line them up with the other cards.

5. Number all the cards so they will be in consecutive order.

6. Proceed in a similar manner to arrange the operations for the other divisions.

CARD METHOD FOR SECURING AN INSTRUCTIONAL ORDER—PRODUCTION OPERATIONS

1. Select a series of typical projects and write the name of each project on a 3″ x 5″ card. A *typical project* is one involving certain basic operations which are to be taught as previously described in Chapter IX. It does not necessarily mean that the projects chosen are the ones that will be made by the students. These projects serve only as a means for arranging the operations in an instructional order. There is a further discussion of projects in Chapter XI.

2. Analyze each project for the operations that must be performed in constructing it. List these operations under each project. See Fig. 6. It is not necessary to arrange the operations in the order they are to be executed in making the project.

3. Prepare a tabulation sheet as shown in Fig. 7.

4. Check each project card and record each operation on the tabulation sheet.

5. Now take the operation cards and arrange them according to the frequency listed on the tabulation sheet. Spread the cards so that those with the greatest frequency are on top and the others fall in their respective positions. If two or more operations show the same frequency of use, arrange these cards so the operations will fall in a logical order of performance. For example, it will be noticed in Fig. 7 that the tabulation sheet shows the same frequency for operations "measure sheetmetal" and "lay out a pattern." Since the operation "measuring" invariably is performed before "laying out a pattern," this operation should be placed ahead of the other.

6. When all the cards have been arranged in their respective order, number each operation card 1, 2, 3, 4, etc.

Project—FLOWER BOX

Operations:

1. Measure sheetmetal
2. Lay out pattern
3. Cut metal with snips
4. File metal
5. Solder sheetmetal
6. Bend metal by hand
7. Bend metal on bar folder
8. Make a single and double hem
9. Cut metal on squaring shears

Project—APRON

Operations

1. Pin pattern on fabric
2. Cut
3. Baste hem
4. Stitch hem
5. Hem ties
6. Baste band and ties
7. Stitch band and ties
8. Pull out bastings
9. Press

Fig. 6. Project Cards Showing the Operations Involved

CHART METHOD FOR SECURING AN INSTRUCTIONAL ORDER

The chart method is somewhat similar to the card technique just described except that the projects and operations are posted on a chart as shown in Fig. 9. The chart method is limited to an analysis in which production type of operations are involved. Here is how the chart is used:

81

1. Lay out a chart as illustrated in Fig. 8. Use a separate chart for each block of operations.

2. List the operations on the left side of the chart. Do not be concerned at this stage about arranging the operations in any particular order. Write down each operation as it is recalled. It is not important if some operations are omitted. They can be added later.

3. Across the top of the chart, list a series of typical projects which are considered suitable for the grade level for which the course of study is being designed.

4. Examine each project and place a check mark after each operation which is involved in making the project. Do this for every project listed. In all probability the projects will disclose the omission of some opera-

OPERATION TABULATION SHEET

Operation	Frequency of Use	Total
Make lap seam	~~IIII~~ 1	6
Make single and double hem	~~IIII~~ ~~IIII~~ 11	12
Measure sheetmetal	~~IIII~~ ~~IIII~~ ~~IIII~~ 1	16
Punch holes	1111	4
Rivet sheetmetal	1	1
Lay out pattern	~~IIII~~ ~~IIII~~ ~~IIII~~ 1	16
Make wire edge	~~IIII~~ 1	6

Fig. 7. Operation Tabulation Chart

tions which were not originally posted. In such a case add the new operation to the bottom of the list.

Occasionally there will be an operation after which no check marks appear. Therefore, additional projects embodying these operations will have to be included. If it appears that the number of projects are too numerous for the time available, then the operations having no check marks may be eliminated. However, if these operations are considered to be important, then one of two things must be done. Either new projects requiring the use of these operations must be substituted for some already listed or a few of the other operations will have to be deleted.

5. Now examine the whole chart. Locate the operations which have full rows of horizontal check marks and transfer them to another similar chart. The operations with full check marks represent the operations that appear in all projects and must be taught first. When several operations have an identical number of check marks, list these operations on the new chart in their correct order of performance.

SHEETMETAL ANALYSIS CHART NO. 1

Operations	Birdhouse	Sugar Scoop	Utility Box	Toy Pail	Flower Box	Wastebasket	Ash Tray	Canteen	Tin Cup	Funnel	Tackle Box	Calendar Holder	Desk Pad	Book Ends	Spice Can Holder	Minnow Bucket	FREQUENCY OF OPERATIONS
Make lap seam	X			X		X				X		X				X	6
Make single and double hem	X			X	X	X	X	X	X		X	X		X	X	X	12
Measure sheetmetal	X	X	X	X	X	X	X	X	X	X	X	X	X	X	X	X	16
Punch holes				X							X	X				X	4
Rivet sheetmetal											X						1
Lay out pattern	X	X	X	X	X	X	X	X	X	X	X	X	X	X	X	X	16
Make wire edge	X			X		X			X		X					X	6
Solder sheetmetal	X	X	X	X	X	X	X	X	X	X	X	X	X	X	X	X	16
Cut on ring and circular shears								X	X						X	X	4
Burr an edge						X	X	X	X								4
Bend metal on brake	X			X		X					X	X		X			6
Drill holes	X			X							X	X				X	5
Cut large holes in metal				X				X			X					X	4
Flange metal				X					X	X	X	X				X	6
Bend metal by hand	X	X	X	X	X	X	X	X	X	X	X	X	X	X	X	X	16
Bend metal on bar folder	X		X	X	X	X	X	X			X	X	X	X	X	X	13
Form sheetmetal				X				X	X	X					X	X	6
Make grooved seam									X	X						X	3
Bead and crimp metal											X					X	2
Cut metal with snips	X	X	X	X	X	X	X	X	X	X	X	X	X	X	X	X	16
Raise metal								X									1
Cut metal on squaring shears	X			X	X	X	X	X			X	X	X	X	X	X	12
Cut metal with chisel	X			X				X			X					X	5
Make double seam						X											1
Make single seam									X	X	X					X	4
File sheetmetal	X	X	X	X	X	X	X	X	X	X	X	X	X	X	X	X	16
Number of Operations in Each Project	14	6	7	18	9	14	10	15	14	11	19	14	8	10	11	21	

Fig. 8. Preliminary Working Chart for Analysis of Operations

SHEETMETAL ANALYSIS CHART NO. 2

Operation	1. Sugar Scoop	2. Utility Box	3. Desk Pad	4. Flower Box	5. Book Ends	6. Ash Tray	7. Funnel	8. Spice Can Holder	9. Calendar Holder	10. Wastebasket	11. Birdhouse	12. Tin Cup	13. Canteen	14. Toy Pail	15. Tackle Box	16. Minnow Bucket
1. Measure sheetmetal	X	X	X	X	X	X	X	X	X	X	X	X	X	X	X	X
2. Layout pattern	X	X	X	X	X	X	X	X	X	X	X	X	X	X	X	X
3. Cut metal with snips	X	X	X	X	X	X	X	X	X	X	X	X	X	X	X	X
4. File metal	X	X	X	X	X	X	X	X	X	X	X	X	X	X	X	X
5. Solder sheetmetal	X	X	X	X	X	X	X	X	X	X	X	X	X	X	X	X
6. Bend metal by hand	X	X	X	X	X	X	X	X	X	X	X	X	X	X	X	X
7. Bend metal on bar folder		X	X	X	X	X		X	X	X		X	X	X	X	X
8. Make single and double hem		X	X					X	X	X	X		X	X	X	X
9. Cut metal on squaring shears				X	X	X	X	X	X				X		X	X
10. Bend metal on brake					X				X						X	X
11. Make lap seam						X	X				X	X	X		X	X
12. Form sheetmetal						X	X			X	X	X	X	X	X	X
13. Flange metal						X	X		X		X	X	X		X	X
14. Make wired edge						X	X	X		X			X	X	X	X
15. Drill holes								X	X		X		X		X	X
16. Cut metal with chisel									X				X		X	X
17. Cut large holes in metal									X		X		X			X
18. Cut on ring and circular shears										X		X	X	X	X	X
19. Burr an edge										X		X	X	X	X	X
20. Make single seam										X		X	X		X	X
21. Punch holes											X		X		X	X
22. Make grooved seam												X	X	X	X	X
23. Bead and crimp metal														X		X
24. Raise metal													X			
25. Make double seam														X		
26. Rivet sheetmetal															X	

Fig. 9. Final Working Chart for Analysis of Operations

6. Transfer the remaining operations to the new chart. The position of these operations should be determined according to the frequency of their check marks.

7. The next step is to organize the projects in their proper order. Unlike operations, the projects must be arranged from the simplest to the most complex. It is considered good pedagogical procedure to start students with projects having the least number of operations. Accordingly, add up the number of check marks in each vertical column. This will produce the number of operations that are involved for each project listed at the top of the chart. Whenever two projects show the same number of operations, check to determine whether or not the operations for these projects are identical. If they show that the same operations are involved, then one of the projects should be eliminated. Remember that projects are the basis for teaching operations, and the only justification for introducing a new project is that it provides a different learning experience. If two projects show identical operations, then it is expedient, during the process of making the analysis, to include only those projects that produce a progressive order of learning.

8. Transfer the names of the projects to the new chart and arrange them according to their number of check marks. Place the name of the project with the least number of marks to the left of the chart and the remaining ones in their corresponding positions.

9. Number the operations in a consecutive order beginning with the first operation on the top of the chart. Do the same with the projects, starting from the left of the chart.

10. Replace the check marks in the correct square after each operation and under each project. If the analysis has been properly made, it should be possible to draw a diagonal line from left to right of the chart with the greatest frequency of check marks above this line. When the check marks are too widely scattered on both sides of the diagonal line, it is a general indication that the instructional order is not too efficient.

DISCUSSION QUESTIONS

1. When arranging operations in an instructional order, what three factors should be taken into consideration?
2. Why is it poor practice to arrange operations on the basis of difficulty?
3. Why must the card method rather than the chart method be used to secure an instructional order when servicing type of operations are involved?
4. What is meant by a typical project? Are these the projects the students will be expected to complete for the course? Explain.

5. In securing an instructional order, what should be the determining criterion when several operations show the same frequency of use?
6. How does the chart method of analysis differ from the card method?
7. What factor should be considered when arranging projects for a proper teaching order?
8. When making an analysis where two typical projects show that identical operations are involved, what is the reasonable procedure to follow?
9. What is meant by a progressive order of learning?
10. How is it possible to determine from the analysis chart whether or not the operations have been arranged to produce an efficient, progressive order of learning?

SPECIAL ASSIGNMENT

Using the operations which you have selected for your course of study, arrange them in an instructional order. Use either the chart or card method.

ADDITIONAL READING

Allen, Charles R., *The Instructor, the Man, and the Job* (Philadelphia: J. B. Lippincott Co., 1919), chaps. IX, X, XI, XII.

Anderson, Miles H., *Teaching Apprentices*, American Technical Society, Chicago: 1949, chap. X.

Bollinger, E. W., and Weaver, G. G., *Occupational Instruction* (New York: Pitman, 1945), chap. VII.

Finsterbach, F. C., "The Time Element in Industrial Arts," *School Shop*, 1947, p. 5.

Friese, John F., *Course Making in Industrial Education* (Peoria, Ill.: Chas. A. Bennett Co., 1946), chap. VIII.

Fryklund, Verne C., *Trade and Job Analysis* (Milwaukee, Wis.: The Bruce Publishing Co., 1947), chap. VI.

Selvidge, R. W., *How to Teach a Trade* (Peoria, Ill.: Chas. A. Bennett Co., 1923), chap. VII.

CHAPTER 11————

Selecting the Work Jobs and Projects

Industrial arts and vocational education courses consist of many activities, but, for the most part, experiences are centered around jobs and projects. Students are given an opportunity to make things, and at the same time learn the real significance of their work as it is related to modern enterprises. The effectiveness of the courses consequently depends considerably on (1) the purposefulness of the manipulative activities, and (2) the extent manual instruction is integrated with the informational subject matter. The main consideration in this chapter will be the vehicles of manipulative instruction, namely, the project or job.

THE SERVICE JOBS

As previously stated, in courses including servicing type of operations, the medium of instruction is the actual execution of these operations. In other words, the operations become the jobs. Once the instructional order is determined, it is a matter of providing the necessary means whereby students can perform these operations.

Servicing type of operations are usually characteristic of such courses as automotive repair, electricity, radio, home mechanics, refrigeration, plumbing, aircraft mechanics, various areas of agriculture, some phases of homemaking and distributive occupations. The following are a few examples of service jobs:

AIRCRAFT MECHANICS

1. Repairing a rib
2. Splicing a cable

3. Patching a tear in fabric
4. Doping a surface
5. Installing a wing
6. Cleaning plexiglass
7. Timing an engine
8. Assembling an engine
9. Compensating a compass
10. Adjusting brakes

ELECTRICAL

1. Wiring a simple lighting system
2. Installing a flush receptacle
3. Testing and replacing fuses
4. Connecting a bell system
5. Wiring a lamp socket
6. Installing a three-way circuit
7. Testing a circuit
8. Installing a fuse box and switch
9. Wiring an appliance plug
10. Making a western union splice

AUTOMOTIVE REPAIR

1. Relining brakes
2. Adjusting toe-in and toe-out
3. Balancing a wheel and tire assembly
4. Installing shock absorbers
5. Replacing rear axle shaft
6. Replacing points
7. Cleaning carbon from cylinder head
8. Removing and installing water pump
9. Installing, adjusting, and testing carburetor
10. Adjusting valve clearance

MERCHANDISING

1. Displaying shirts and ties
2. Showing shirt on a shirt-easel
3. Displaying neckware
4. Arranging hosiery
5. Folding handkerchiefs
6. Displaying suits
7. Creasing the hat
8. Spacing luggage

DAIRY CATTLE HUSBANDRY

1. Raising dairy calves and heifers
2. Feeding cattle
3. Estimating weight of cattle
4. Dehorning cattle
5. Milking

BEAUTY CULTURE

1. Styling hair
2. Cleaning and brushing hair
3. Cleansing skin
4. Plucking eyebrows
5. Applying lipstick
6. Manicuring

MAKING SERVICING JOBS PRACTICAL

If the servicing jobs are to provide the necessary inducement for maximum student interest and learning, they must be taught under conditions approximating as nearly as possible those found in industry.[1] This is particularly important for trade classes where occupational competency is the desired goal. Even though operations may have the semblance of practicality, if they are taught in a situation where the setting is not conducive to good work, the equipment is not up to date, and the tools are inadequate, the operations lose their true value and the jobs become meaningless, routine assignments. Sometimes it is impossible in a school shop or laboratory to provide an appropriate teaching atmosphere. It may be difficult, for example, to duplicate working conditions that are found in an automotive service station. But if automotive repair is to be taught effectively, all the selected operations must be performed with equipment that is usually found in service shops. Demonstrating with obsolete equipment and having students work on jobs that are "makeshift" in nature is not the proper way to achieve occupational competency.

PRODUCTION PROJECTS

The project is the main vehicle for teaching production operations. It represents a concrete object to be made.

The introduction of the project in American industrial education programs was largely the result of a change in educational philosophy. During the early manual training era, instruction was influenced greatly by the Russian system of tool exercises.[2] The advent of the Swedish Sloyd movement and the introduction of new concepts of manual arts, later known as industrial arts, were instrumental in promoting a new in-

---

[1] E. W. Bollinger and G. G. Weaver, *Occupational Instruction* (New York: Pitman, 1945), p. 52.

[2] Gordon O. Wilber, *Industrial Arts in General Education* (Scranton, Pa.: International Textbook Co., 1948), p. 145.

structional trend.[3] The meaningless exercises gradually were eliminated from the program and students were given an opportunity to work on more useful articles.

The utilization of the project as the instructional medium has done a great deal to stimulate student interest in both industrial arts and vocational courses. Although this is particularly significant insofar as industrial arts classes are concerned, the project has also become an important motivating factor in trade courses where mastery of skills plays an essential role.

CRITERIA FOR SELECTING PROJECTS

When selecting projects for any instructional program, the following points should be kept in mind:

1. **The project must incorporate operations to be taught.** Since the basic operations are primarily the main core of the teachable content, the projects selected should embody these necessary operations. Accordingly, each project must be carefully analyzed so there is assurance that the desired ends are attainable.

2. **The project must be of interest to the student.** Too often projects are chosen by the teacher either because they seem appropriate for the course or because their construction is easily controlled for a given situation. Little or no consideration is given to whether or not they may be of interest to the students. Each student is required to make what the teacher suggests even though the designated project has no personal appeal to him. As a result, the completion of such a project generally becomes a necessary chore, something to be done in order to satisfy the requirements of the course. There is nothing as devastating to pupil morale as being confined to an uninteresting task.

3. **The project must possess utility value.** Next to having student appeal, a project should be practical, that is, have some useful purpose. The student should be able to use the finished project as a personal possession or take it home as a useful household article. If more teachers took an inventory of what students did with the things made, probably more attention would be given to this factor of utility value.

4. **Each project should introduce new instructional material.** The function of any course is to provide a variety of experiences. Unless each project contributes some new learning process, the time spent on it may be questionable. In the final analysis it is not important what or how

[3] John F. Friese, *Course Making in Industrial Education* (Peoria, Ill.: Chas. A. Bennett Co., 1946), p. 45.

many things a student makes, but rather on how varied his experiences have been. Hence, it is expedient to study carefully each task assigned to the student so he will obtain the maximum educational value from the course.

In addition, each project should permit an opportunity to apply the things learned in preceding projects. It is by means of this repetitive process that skills are developed. Since high degrees of skills in performing operations are essential in vocational courses, there must of necessity be greater provisions for repetitive work than in industrial arts courses.

5. **The project must be within the student's ability to make.** It is very disheartening for any person to work on a job that inevitably leads to failure. Projects which are too large, or require workmanship beyond a student's ability, should be avoided. Likewise, precaution must be taken not to assign tasks that are too easy. The work must offer a challenge if interest is to be maintained.

6. **A project must be well designed.** The atrocities that sometimes come from school shops and laboratories are often an indictment against the program. Students should be required to use good principles of design in making projects. Actually the shop teacher should be as concerned with teaching basic principles of good design as the art teacher.

7. **The project must permit completion within a reasonable time limit.** The interest span of most students is not too long. Enthusiasm soon wanes and eventually may cease entirely. The project that was started with such spirited interest loses its appeal if it takes too long to finish. It is far better to have a student work on several projects during the semester than to work on one or two projects that require the entire semester to complete.

8. **The project must be reasonable in cost.** This is especially true if students have to pay for the material used. The expense in building projects requiring costly or a great deal of material is generally prohibitive for most students.

STUDENT SELECTION OF PROJECTS

A problem that often disturbs the teacher is the amount of leeway students should be given in making projects of their own choice. Three practices are usually followed. With one plan no choice whatsoever is permitted. The teacher simply selects what he considers to be the appropriate things to make for the predetermined operations, and all students are expected to complete these projects. This plan becomes very easy to administer, especially after the teacher has prepared all the project plans and other instructional material. However, such a plan offers limited educational values to the students.

Another practice is to allow the students to make anything they please. Aside from the fact that this program is difficult to administer, it does not permit the organization of any concrete body of instructional material for guided learning. Students need some direction, and it is the teacher's responsibility to provide an educational setting that enables students to pursue an organized plan of instruction. Where students are allowed to follow their own inclinations by working on projects that may momentarily suit their whims or interest, learning often becomes secondary in importance.

The third practice is somewhat of a compromise between the first two. With this plan the teacher selects a series of typical projects which incorporate the desired teachable material as described in Chapter IX. Then alternate projects are listed under each typical project from which students may make a choice. Each of the alternate projects provides the same learning experiences as the typical projects. The feature of such a plan is that the teacher has charted the course of instruction to be followed, yet the student's interests are still recognized.

LISTING THE PROJECTS FOR THE COURSE OF STUDY

In preparing a course of study, the alternate projects should temporarily be listed on 3″ x 5″ cards. If the card method of operation analysis is used, write the names of the alternate projects on the back of each card containing the name of the typical project. See Fig. 10.

With the chart method of operation analysis, simply transfer each typical project from the chart onto 3″ x 5″ cards. Then list the alternate projects on these cards.

DISCUSSION QUESTIONS

1. How are service jobs differentiated from production jobs?
2. Why is it so important for the teacher to make service jobs as practical as possible?
3. Why is teaching exclusively by the exercise method generally considered impractical for good learning?
4. Is there any difference between a project and a job? Explain.
5. What are some of the important factors to be considered when selecting projects?
6. Why is it poor practice for the teacher to select all the projects without taking into account student interest?
7. How can a teacher ascertain if the projects have utility value?
8. To what extent should repetitive work be provided? How can this best be done?

9. Why should a student be discouraged from making a project that is beyond his capacity? How can this be done without "killing" student interest?
10. To what extent should students be allowed to select their own projects?

TYPICAL PROJECT
Utility Box

<u>Operations</u>

1. Laying out a pattern
2. Cutting metal with hand snips
3. Filing sheetmetal
4. Bending sheetmetal
5. Riveting sheetmetal
6. Soldering
7. Drilling holes

Front

ALTERNATE PROJECTS

1. Soap box
2. Sugar scoop
3. Flower pot
4. Birdhouse
5. Feed scoop
6. Desk pad
7. Book ends
8. Spice can rack

Back

Fig. 10.   Listing Alternate Projects on 3″ x 5″ Cards

11. What is the limitation of the plan whereby students may make whatever they wish?
12. What is the difference between a typical project and an alternate project?

SPECIAL ASSIGNMENT

Select the necessary projects for your course of study and list them on 3″ x 5″ cards. List several alternate projects for each typical project chosen.

ADDITIONAL READING

Bollinger, E. W., and Weaver, G. G., *Occupational Instruction* (New York: Pitman, 1945), chap. VI.

Drazek, Stanley J., "Live Jobs Wake Up Lagging Automotive Class," *School Shop*, September, 1944, p. 9.

Friese, John F., *Course Making in Industrial Education* (Peoria, Ill.: Chas. A. Bennett Co., 1946), chap. IV.

Sotzin, H. A., "Making Woodworking Challenging," *School Shop*, April, 1951, p. 17.

Wilber, Gordon O., *Industrial Arts in General Education* (Scranton, Pa.: International Textbook Co., 1948), chap. X.

CHAPTER 12 ─────────

Analyzing a Course for Its Related Information

Thus far the instructional analysis has dealt with the manipulative aspects of the course content. The next phase of the analysis is to ascertain the nature and scope of the informational material. This material is generally referred to as related information. It is the information the student should know in order to perform the manipulative work intelligently.

KINDS OF RELATED INFORMATION

There are several kinds of related information associated with any industrial arts and vocational education courses. These may be classified as general, technical, socio-economic, safety, and occupational information.

General information is information which is desirable for a student to know, but it is not directly connected with any phase of the manipulative work. It is material which gives the student an understanding of some of the significant relationships of their instructional areas with occupational developments. This information is usually concerned with the manufacture of materials, inventions of tools and machines, production methods, and industrial organization. Here are a few examples of general information topics:

1. Manufacture of iron and steel
2. How lumber is produced
3. Origin of the lathe
4. Development of the production system of manufacturing

5. Edison and his inventions
6. How modern industry operates
7. Prehistoric farm implements
8. Early methods of cooking
9. Modern production of beauty aids
10. How fertilizers are made

Technical information is material which helps a student form correct judgments and make proper decisions in performing the jobs or operations. It deals with specifications of materials, fabricating procedures, tools, and machines. The following are a few examples of technical information topics:

1. Types and sizes of sheetmetal
2. Solders and fluxes
3. Kinds of abrasives
4. Hacksaws and blades
5. Types of files
6. Fits, limits, and tolerances
7. Taps and dies
8. Areas and circumferences
9. Taper calculations
10. Designing projects
11. Wood finishing products
12. Types of shampoos
13. Composition of fertilizers
14. Kinds of fabrics

Socio-economic information is information which helps a student understand how industry functions in a world in which people live and work. Such information is probably given less attention in school work than is warranted. This is regrettable because the complexity of industry today requires all workers to have a much greater knowledge of socio-economic problems than at any previous time in history.

Examples of information topics concerned with the socio-economic aspects of industry are:

1. Workmen's Compensation
2. Social Security
3. Trade Unions
4. Labor Laws
5. Federal and State Legislation on Wages and Hours
6. Quantity Production and Cost
7. Unemployment Insurance

Safety information is information dealing with safety practices in the home and shop. The need for stressing this type of information in the school shop or laboratory is apparent. Industry places a great premium on safety. Teachers likewise should exert the utmost effort to have students develop good safety habits. Reference to safety information should not be confused with the specific precautions that must be taught while demonstrating operations. In addition to these safety practices, there are general safety topics which students should be given an opportunity to discuss. Here are a few such safety information topics:

1. First aid
2. Importance of safety in the school shop
3. What industry thinks of safety
4. Basic safety practices to observe around the home
5. General conduct in the school shop or laboratory

Occupational information is guidance information dealing with the selection of and preparation for an occupation. It also includes such topics as how to keep a job, employment opportunities, compensation, and so on. The following example shows the nature of occupational information topics:

Sheetmetal Occupation

1. Types of sheetmetal occupations
2. Working conditions and compensation
3. Preparation required for securing a job
4. Opportunities for advancement
5. Employee-employer relations
6. Types and locations of sheetmetal industries

HOW TO IDENTIFY RELATED INFORMATION

Related information should not be confused with the term "related subjects." When organized courses such as drawing, shop mathematics, and shop science are taught as separate courses, they are generally known as "related subjects." Related information, on the other hand, is taught by the teacher as an essential part of his course. Related subjects are often identified with federally reimbursed classes.

Related information should not be mistaken for knowledge that is closely integrated with teaching the operations. Fryklund[1] refers to this information as auxiliary knowledge. For example, auxiliary information involves brief instructions on why a tool is used in a certain way, or why a step in an operation is performed in a particular manner, or safety precautions to observe while performing the operation, and other similar in-

---

[1] Verne C. Fryklund, *Trade and Job Analysis* (Milwaukee, Wis.: The Bruce Publishing Co., 1947), p. 57.

formation which must be taught as the operation is demonstrated. Usually discussion of this kind of information is very short. It covers only those details necessary to give meaning to the operation that is being demonstrated.

Regular information topics should not be considered as incidental instructional material. They should carry the same status in a course as the operations. Since they have their own entity, related information topics should be taught as separate lessons. Some of the information topics must, of necessity, be taught before the operations are demonstrated. When topics cannot be tied in with any definite operation, they can be taught at any convenient time during the course.

The mistake should never be made of teaching related information along with the demonstration. As a rule, the operation being demonstrated is difficult enough for the students to learn. Introducing factual material at this stage only complicates the learning process. Furthermore, when students are watching a demonstration, they are not interested in information that does not apply to what is being shown.

SELECTING THE INFORMATION TOPICS

The main criteria in the selection of information topics are the appropriateness of the material for the course and the length of time available for teaching the course. In each instance the question should be asked, "Is this information valuable? Does it enhance the course? Does it achieve some of the desirable objectives?" Unless related information topics contribute significantly to the attainment of some definite aspect of the work, they should not be included.

In proceeding to select the information topics, concentrate on one category of information and then go on to the next. For example, make a list of all the general information topics, then do the same for the technical information, and so on. Use 3″ x 5″ cards and limit one topic to each card. It may be necessary to consult textbooks, periodicals, and other literature to get complete coverage of all essential topics. A point to keep in mind is that there need not be an information topic for each operation. Some courses, because of the amount of information required, will have many more information topics than others. Once the listing is done, analyze each topic to be sure it is appropriate to the course.

ARRANGING THE RELATED INFORMATION TOPICS

The next step is to organize the information topics in some logical instructional order. A convenient way to do this is to spread out the op-

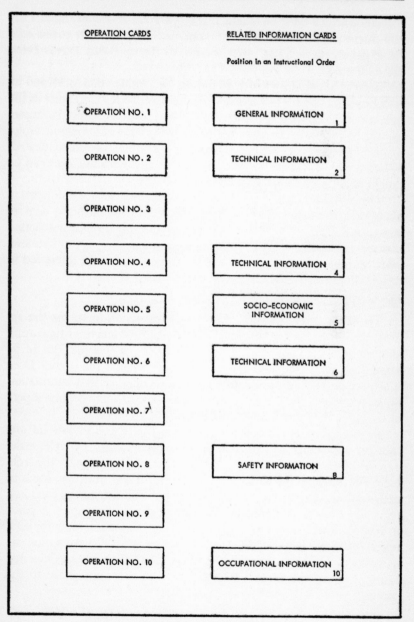

Fig. 11. Arranging Related Information Topics

eration cards in their sequential teaching order. Then place the technical information cards alongside those operation cards that have a close relationship. Arrange the remaining information cards in any position which seems appropriate for effective teaching. See Fig. 11. Since the general, socio-economic safety, and occupational information topics are not allied with any particular operation, their location in an instructional order is largely a matter of personal judgment.

Now number the information topics so as to record their position. This will simplify the procedure later when the entire course of study is assembled.

DISCUSSION QUESTIONS

1. What is meant by related information? Of what significance is it in an instructional program?
2. What is the difference between general and technical information?
3. What is socio-economic information? Why should this information be stressed?
4. Why should safety information be included in a course? With what should safety information deal?
5. Why is it important to include occupational information in a course? What are some of the topics that should be discussed when covering occupational information?
6. In what way do related subjects differ from related information?
7. How can auxiliary knowledge be distinguished from genuine information topics?
8. Why is it impractical to teach related information when demonstrating an operation?
9. Should there be an information topic for each listed operation? Explain.
10. When an information topic cannot be tied in with an operation, where should it be listed in an instructional order?

SPECIAL ASSIGNMENT

Select the related information topics for your course, and arrange them in an instructional order.

ADDITIONAL READING

Bollinger, E. W., and Weaver, G. G., *Occupational Instruction* (New York: Pitman, 1945), chaps. VIII, IX.

Friese, John F., *Course Making in Industrial Education* (Peoria, Ill.: Chas. A. Bennett Co., 1946), chap. X.

Fryklund, Verne C., *Trade and Job Analysis* (Milwaukee, Wis.: The Bruce Publishing Co., 1947), chap. V.

Mohn, Harvey A., "Method of Correlating Related Technology and

Shop Practice," *Industrial Arts and Vocational Education,* April, 1951, p. 150.

Sechrest, Chas. H., "A Method for Teaching General Information in Industrial Arts," *School Shop,* 1948, p. 5.

Smith, Lester C., "Correlating Shopwork with Other Subjects," *School Shop,* April, 1944, p. 3.

Wilber, Gordon O., *Industrial Arts in General Education* (Scranton, Pa.: International Textbook Co., 1948), chap. VI.

CHAPTER 13 ————

Analyzing Operations and Related Information

The material which a teacher selects for a single presentation to the students is referred to as a lesson. This material may deal with the teaching of a skill lesson or an information lesson. A skill lesson is one involving the demonstration of an operation. An information lesson is one dealing with the teaching of related information.

To present a lesson effectively, a teacher must outline carefully the material to be taught. Thus, the operation to be demonstrated must be analyzed to make certain that no part of the operation is omitted and that all the steps presented are in a logical order. The same is true of the information lesson; the material must be carefully analyzed so as to include all the pertinent facts.

In preparing a course of study, the writer may wish to include a complete analysis of each operation and information topic. Many teachers prefer to identify the operations and information topics only in the course of study and record the analysis on separate cards. The advantage of having such material on cards is that these cards may be used conveniently as lesson plans. When prepared in this manner, they can easily be pulled out of the card file and used whenever the lesson is to be presented. In this chapter instructions will be given on how operations and related information topics should be analyzed into their appropriate steps.

ANALYZING OPERATIONS

An operation to be demonstrated properly must follow a certain sequential order. In other words, the teacher must show what is to be done step by step, each step being demonstrated in its natural order of performance. These steps are commonly referred to as performing steps.

There are two types of performing steps—the doing steps and those involving auxiliary knowledge. As it was pointed out in a previous chapter, auxiliary knowledge is simply that information which explains why or how a step is performed, or the care of a tool, or a safety precaution. It is a type of information which can be presented quickly in a few words without disrupting the continuity of the doing steps.

The listing of the performing steps should be done in telegraphic form; that is, complete sentences are unnecessary. Only sufficient words are needed to remind the teacher of the correct order of the steps. Several examples of how an operation should be outlined follow.

Example No. 1—Sheetmetal

How To Cut Holes with a Circle Cutter

1. Locate center
2. Adjust crossarm on cutter
3. Clamp cutter in chuck of drill press
4. Fasten metal—safety precaution
5. Be sure and use hardwood backing block
6. Lower cutter with pilot drill in punched hole
7. Remove burr with file

Example No. 2—Benchmetal

How To Drill Holes

1. Center punch hole
2. Select correct drill size
3. Note: stress importance of sharp drill
4. Insert drill in chuck
5. Clamp work in vise
6. Adjust belt for correct speed
7. Start motor and drill
8. Use lubricant
9. Avoid too much pressure
10. Reduce pressure as drill cuts through metal

Example No. 3--Woodworking

How To Sand--Wood Surfaces

1. Select correct sandpaper
2. Tear sheet
3. Wrap sandpaper over block
4. Sand back and forth--flat surface
5. Sand with grain; do not use circular motion
6. End grain; sand one direction

Example No. 4--Electricity

How To Attach a Plug

1. Remove outer covering on wire--about three-fourths inch
2. Cut insulation with slanting cuts
3. Do not cut straight around wire
4. Thread cord through cap
5. Tie underwriters' knot
6. Loosen screws in plug cap
7. Pull knot tight into top of cap
8. Wrap wire around plug part
9. Tighten screws upon wire

Example No. 5--Cooking

How To Make Spanish Rice

1. Heat shortening in heavy frying pan
2. Fry peppers and onions in shortening
3. Caution: Remove as soon as delicately colored
4. Add rice
5. Add seasonings, tomatoes, sugar
6. Cover and simmer until tender
7. Add water or stock to prevent burning
8. Cook for about $1\frac{1}{4}$ hours

Example No. 6--Beauty Culture

How To Apply Cleansing Cream

1. Remove surface dirt
2. Apply cream with light strokes

3. Caution—never use rubbing or downward motion
4. Start at base of neck and proceed to jawbones, nose, cheeks, temple, forehead
5. Remove cream with tissues
6. Place warm towels on face
7. Apply soap and rinse in warm, then cold water
8. Pat face dry
9. Apply soothing lotion

ANALYZING RELATED INFORMATION TOPICS

Related information topics should be carefully outlined to show the nature and scope of material to be covered. Standard outlining procedures should be used as shown in the following examples.

Example No. 1

TECHNICAL INFORMATION

Twist Drills

I. Parts of a drill
   A. Shank
   B. Body
   C. Point
      1. Lip clearance
      2. Correct angle

II. Sizes of drills
   A. Numerical
   B. Alphabetical
   C. Fractional

III. Types of drills
   A. Carbon
   B. High speeds
   C. Types of shanks

Example No. 2

TECHNICAL INFORMATION

Files

I. Parts of file

II. Type of cuts
   A. Single cut
   B. Double cut

III. Coarseness of cut
   A. Rough
   B. Coarse
   C. Bastard
   D. Second
   E. Smooth

IV. Kinds of files
   A. Mill
   B. Flat
   C. Hand
   D. Half-round
   E. Three-square
   F. Square
   G. Round
   H. Special files

V. Selecting correct file

Example No. 3

GENERAL INFORMATION

Manufacture of Iron

I. Importance of iron
   A. Discovery
      1. Early history
      2. How used
   B. Examples of use today

II. Types of ores
   A. Hematite
   B. Limonite
   C. Magnetite
   D. Siderite

III. Mining ore
   A. Location of deposits
   B. Method of mining
      1. Open-pit
      2. Underground

Example No. 4

GENERAL INFORMATION

Fashion Facts

I. Style and fashion
   A. Factors influencing style
   B. Difference between style and fashion

II. Cycle of fashion
   A. Inspiration of modern modes
   B. Costumes in ancient times
      1. Egyptian
      2. Classical Greek
      3. Roman
      4. Costumes during Middle Ages
      5. Costumes during the Renaissance
   C. Costumes in modern times
      1. English influence
      2. French influence
      3. American influence

Example No. 5

TECHNICAL INFORMATION

Fibers and Fabrics

I. Types of fibers
   A. Cotton
   B. Linen
   C. Wool
   D. Silk
   E. Rayon
   F. Synthetics

Example No. 6

SOCIO-ECONOMIC INFORMATION

Social Security

I. Purpose of Social Security

II. Persons eligible
   A. Classification
   B. How to determine if eligible

106

II. Fabric construction
  A. Weaving
  B. Knitting
  C. Felting
  D. Braiding

III. Design in fabrics
  A. Forming designs
  B. Applying designs

IV. Fabric finishes

III. Social Security benefits
  A. As protection
  B. Retirement

IV. Payment
  A. Government obligation
  B. Individual obligation
  C. Employer obligation
  D. Amount

V. Submitting claim

Example No. 7

OCCUPATIONAL INFORMATION

Garment Trade

I. Type of work performed
  A. Classification of workers
  B. Types of industries

II. Training required
  A. Length of training
  B. Where secured
  C. Education needed

III. Compensation

IV. Physical requirements

DISCUSSION QUESTIONS

1. What is meant by a lesson?
2. What is the difference between a skill and an information lesson?
3. Why should an operation be broken down into performing steps?
4. How can you tell the difference between an actual operation and a performing step?
5. What is meant by auxiliary knowledge?
6. How does auxiliary knowledge differ from related information?

SPECIAL ASSIGNMENT

Analyze several operations and related information topics. If you plan to include these details in your course of study, it will be necessary that this analysis be carried out for all operations and information topics.

ADDITIONAL READING

Bollinger, E. W., and Weaver, G. G., *Occupational Instruction* (New York: Pitman, 1945), chap. IX.

Fryklund, Verne C., *Trade and Job Analysis* (Milwaukee, Wis.: Bruce Publishing Co., 1947), chap. 8.

Leighbody, Gerald B., *Methods of Teaching Industrial Subjects* (Albany: Delmar, 1946), chap. II.

Selvidge, R. W., and Fryklund, Verne C., *Principles of Trade and Industrial Teaching* (Peoria, Ill.: Chas. A. Bennett Co., 1946), chaps. VII, VIII.

CHAPTER **14**————————

Assembling the Course of Study

The material which is to be included in a course of study was discussed in the preceding chapters. In this chapter instructions will be found on how the various phases can be arranged into an integrated course of study.

The content of most courses of study is assembled either on 8½ x 11 paper or 5 x 8 cards. Both of these plans will be discussed. However, no attempt will be made to justify the merits or limitations of either plan. The individual instructor will have to use his own judgment as to which form will best suit his needs. The important factor is the use of some format that will readily disclose the relationship of all parts of the course of study.

ASSEMBLING THE COURSE ON 8½ x 11 PAPER

When the material is typed on 8½ x 11 sheets, it is recommended that the sequence of the various sections of the course of study be arranged as follows:

TITLE PAGE (see Fig. 12). This page should contain the following information:

1. Name of the course
2. Name of the person who prepared the course of study
3. Name of the school
4. Date the course of study was prepared

INTRODUCTORY STATEMENT (see Fig. 13). Section I of the course of study should present the introductory statement as discussed in Chapter IV.

COURSE OF STUDY

FOR

INDUSTRIAL ARTS GENERAL SHOP

(9th Grade)

J. W. Smith

Painesville High School

November, 1953

Fig. 12. Title Page

SECTION I

INTRODUCTION

I

II

Fig. 13. Section I of Course of Study

TABLE OF CONTENTS (see Fig. 14). The Table of Contents should be Section II of the course of study. Completion of this section may have to be delayed until all the other parts of the course are assem-

SECTION II

TABLE OF CONTENTS

	Page
I. Introduction	2
II. Plan of Instructional Practices	3
III. Educational Philosophy	6
IV. Specific Course Objectives	10
V. Course Outline	12

Divisions of Course

	Weeks	Page
Woodwork	5	12
Metalwork	5	20
Electricity	3	30
Plastics	2	40
Aviation	2	50

Fig. 14. Section II of Course of Study

SECTION III

PLAN OF INSTRUCTIONAL PRACTICES

I. Introduction

II. Teaching Methods

III. Grading Students

Fig. 15. Section III of Course of Study

bled. The Table of Contents should include the title of each section of the course of study, the main divisions of the course, and the page number where each new section begins.

INSTRUCTIONAL PRACTICES (see Fig. 15). A description of the instructional practices which are to be used in teaching the course should be Section III of the course of study. The amount of detail to be shown will be governed largely by how comprehensive the instructor

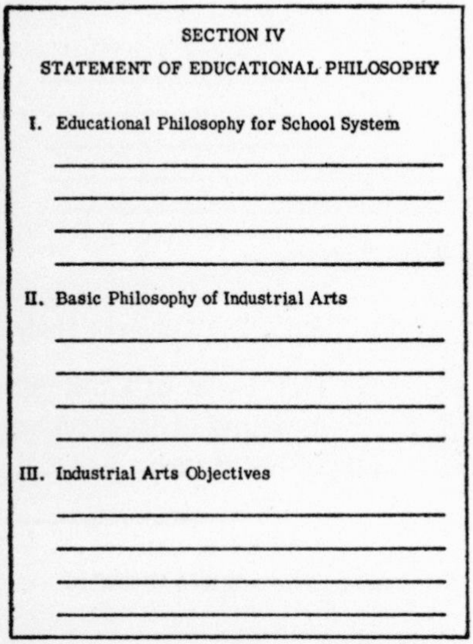
SECTION IV

STATEMENT OF EDUCATIONAL PHILOSOPHY

I. Educational Philosophy for School System

II. Basic Philosophy of Industrial Arts

III. Industrial Arts Objectives

Fig. 16. Section IV of Course of Study

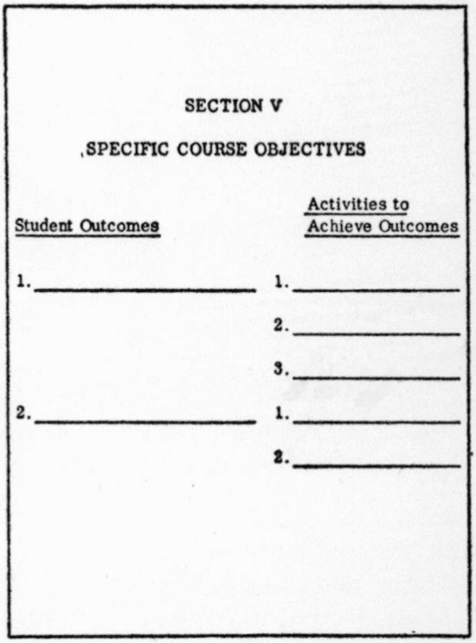
SECTION V

SPECIFIC COURSE OBJECTIVES

Student Outcomes — Activities to Achieve Outcomes

1. — 1. 2. 3.

2. — 1. 2.

Fig. 17. Section V of Course of Study

wants to make the course of study. In general, it should describe some of the important practices as discusssed in Chapter V.

STATEMENT OF EDUCATIONAL PHILOSOPHY (see Fig. 16). Section IV should contain a brief statement of the educational philosophy of the school system as well as the basic philosophy, with its supporting objectives, for the specific subject area (see Chapter VI).

SPECIFIC COURSE OBJECTIVES (see Fig. 17). Section V of the course of study should include the specific course objectives to be achieved and the activities to be provided as a means of attaining the outcomes discussed in Chapter VII. The activities later will be incorporated in another section in order to integrate them with the main body of the course of study.

DIVISION I—WOODWORK—Four Weeks

Unit I

OPERATIONS	PROJECTS	RELATED INFORMATION	SPECIAL ACTIVITIES	INSTRUCTIONAL AIDS
1. Measure with rule	1. Cribbage board	1. Types of woods	1. Student personnel organization	1. Text—Instructional Units in Hand Woodwork—Brown and Tustison
2. Make a layout	Alternate Jobs	2. Types of saws	2. Field trip to saw-mill	
3. Saw to line	a. Bread board	3. Types of planes		2. Chart—samples of sandpaper
4. Square a board	b. Writing board	4. Sandpaper		3. Panel—samples of wood
5. Cut a chamfer	c. Clothesline holder			4. Movie—Lumbering
6. Sand a surface	d. Hot plate holder			
7. Drill and bore holes				

Fig. 18. Course-of-Study Format

FORMATS FOR LISTING THE MAIN BODY OF THE COURSE OF STUDY. Section VI consists of the main body of the course of study. This section should include the operations, projects, or jobs, related information, special activities, and instructional aids. All of

DIVISION I—WOODWORK—Four Weeks	
Unit I	
Operations	Projects

1. Measure with rule
2. Make a layout
3. Saw to line
4. Square a board
5. Cut a chamfer
6. Sand a surface
7. Drill and bore holes
	1. Cribbage Board
	
	Alternate Jobs
	
	  a) Bread board
	  b) Writing board
	  c) Clothesline holder
	  d) Hot plate holder

Related Information	Special Activities	Instructional Aids
1. Types of woods 2. Types of saws 3. Types of planes 4. Sandpaper	1. Student personnel organization 2. Field trip to sawmill	1. Text—Instructional Units in Hand Woodwork—Brown and Tustison 2. Chart—samples of sandpaper 3. Chart—samples of wood 4. Movie—"Lumbering"

Fig. 19. Course-of-Study Format

the information for these items should be transcribed from the cards previously prepared to one of the formats illustrated in Figs. 18, 19, or 20. The format to use will depend on personal choice to a large extent. Some people like to compile their course of study in column form, the columns running across the length of the page as shown in Fig. 18. Others find it

DIVISION I—WOODWORK—Four Weeks

Unit I

Operations

1. Measure with rule
2. Make a layout
3. Saw to line
4. Square a board
5. Cut a chamfer
6. Sand a surface
7. Drill and bore holes

Projects

1. Cribbage board

   Alternate Jobs

   a) Bread board
   b) Writing board
   c) Clothesline holder
   d) Hot plate holder

Related Information

1. Types of woods
2. Types of saws
3. Types of planes
4. Sandpaper

Special Activities

1. Student personnel organization
2. Field trip to sawmill

Instructional Aids

1. Text—Instructional Units in Hand Woodwork—Brown and Tustison
2. Chart—Samples of sandpaper
3. Panel—Samples of wood
4. Movie—"Lumbering"

Fig. 20.   Course-of-Study Format

more convenient to arrange their material in chart form as illustrated in Fig. 19. Still others prefer to use a regular outline form as shown in Fig. 20. In each case, it will be noticed that the relationship of the operations, projects, related information, special activities, and instructional aids is maintained.

Operations: Under this heading list all the operations in their logical teaching sequence. The listing may be confined to merely naming the operation or, as mentioned in Chapter XIII, the operating steps may also be included under each operation (see Fig. 21).

Projects: Under this heading include the selected typical projects as well as the alternate projects.

Related Information: Under this heading list the related information topics. As in the case of the operations, only the title of the information topics may be shown or a complete outline of each topic may be included as discussed in Chapter XIII. It is not necessary to identify each information topic as to its general classification, that is, whether it is general, technical, socio-economic, safety, or guidance, unless one specifically wishes to do so.

Special Activities: This column should contain the activities listed in Section VI of the course of study (see Chapter VII). If these activities can be associated with specific related information topics, operations, or jobs, they should be located near this instructional material; otherwise, they may be scattered throughout the course wherever their introduction may seem most appropriate.

Instructional Aids. Under this heading include specific titles of textbooks, movies, film strips, charts, models, mock-ups, and other aids that will be employed in teaching. In each instance, it is necessary to identify clearly the aid to be employed. For example, if a movie is to be used to teach the related information topic, "Manufacture of Aluminum," the exact title of the movie should be shown. If a chart or model is to be used, its identity should be apparent. The aids should be placed as near as possible to the instructional material that is to be taught.

Format of Course of Study with Servicing Operations. The same formats may be used for courses of study with servicing operations. However, since the servicing operations are the actual jobs to be performed, the column headed "Operations" need not be included (see Fig. 22).

UNIT OF INSTRUCTION

During the arrangement of the material under the various headings, it is frequently desirable to group the content into convenient units of

SHEETMETAL
Unit I

OPERATIONS	PROJECTS	RELATED INFORMATION	SPECIAL ACTIVITIES	INSTRUCTIONAL AIDS
1. Measuring Sheetmetal a. Use U.S. standard gage b. Check edge c. Insert gage over metal d. 18-gage metal, less than 16 2. Layout Pattern a. Draw pattern on paper b. Cut paper outline c. Place pattern in economical position d. Use pencil for tracing e. Trace pattern 3. Cut Metal with Snips a. Select correct snips b. Mark line to be cut c. Watch finger position d. Hold snips in correct position e. Cut small section at a time 4. Solder Sheetmetal a. Clean area b. Tin copper c. Spread flux d. Tack seam e. Solder edge	1. Sugar Scoop Alternate Projects a. Feed scoop b. Box c. Toy shovel	1. Galvanized Iron a. Types b. Uses c. Gages d. Determining costs 2. Aluminum a. Types b. Uses c. Gages 3. Tin Plate a. Types b. Uses c. Sizes	1. Set up a student personnel organization 2. Organize a student planning committee	1. Text — Basic Sheetmetal Practice —Giachino 2. Student study guides 3. Student project planning sheets 4. Movie — "Manufacturing of Aluminum"

Fig. 21. Course-of-Study Format

instruction. The project or job usually can be used as a dividing guide to identify the unit. All the operations, related information, special activities, and instructional aids related to the project can then be placed together to form a unit of instruction. By studying the examples shown in Figs. 18, 19, and 20, this organization will be clarified.

BEAUTY CULTURE UNIT II			
Jobs	Related Information	Special Activities	Instructional Order
1. Washing hair 2. Drying hair 3. Waving hair	1. Soaps 2. Hair shampoos	1. Visit to beauty parlor 2. Make a collection of pictures showing different hair styles	1. Text—Your Clothes and Personality— Ryan

Fig. 22. Course-of-Study Format Having Servicing Operations

It is generally advisable to start each new unit of the outline on a separate page. Doing this will help maintain the identity of the unit. Moreover, it will simplify the task of making revisions without having to retype the entire course of study.

ASSEMBLING THE COURSE OF STUDY ON 5" x 8" CARDS

Some teachers prefer to compile their course of study on 5" x 8" cards. Different colored cards are used to record the various sections of the course of study. For example, this arrangement may be followed:

White cards—Introductory statement, instructional practices, educational philosophy, etc.

Gray cards—Operations

Blue cards—Projects or jobs

Yellow cards—Related information

Green cards—Special activities

Red cards—Instructional aids

Each card should be clearly identified with a heading, as Jobs, Operations, Related Information, and so on. Space should be provided to record the division and the unit of the course as shown in Fig. 23. The instructional material previously prepared is then transferred to these cards. As with the other course of study formats, the job can serve as the

JOBS	Division— Woodwork
	Unit No. —

1. _____

Alternate Jobs
_____
_____
_____
_____

OPERATIONS	Division—
	Unit No. —

1. _____
2. _____
3. _____
4. _____

RELATED INFORMATION	Division—
	Unit No. —

_____
_____
_____
_____
_____

SPECIAL ACTIVITIES	Division—
	Unit No. —

_____
_____
_____
_____

INSTRUCTIONAL AIDS	Division—
	Unit No. —

Textbook
_____

Chart

Movies
_____

Fig. 23. Various 5″ x 8″ Cards for Course of Study

unit of instruction. Tabs can be placed over the job cards for ease in identifying each unit.

SPECIAL ASSIGNMENT

Select one of the formats described in this chapter and assemble your course of study.

ADDITIONAL READING

Anderson, Miles, *Teaching Apprentices* (Chicago: American Technical Society, 1950), chap. X.

Bollinger, E. W., and Weaver, G. G., *Occupational Instruction* (New York: Pitman, 1945), chap. IV.

Friese, John F., *Course Making in Industrial Education* (Peoria, Ill.: Chas. A. Bennett Co., 1946), chap. III.

CHAPTER 15 ————————

Instruction Sheets

Perhaps no greater influence has been exerted on methods of teaching industrial arts and vocational education than that of R. W. Selvidge.[1] As one of the early pioneers in industrial teaching, Selvidge emphasized the use of instruction sheets. Today many teachers still regard teacher-made individual instruction sheets as valuable instructional aids. Although industrial arts teachers are giving less attention to such instruction sheets, nevertheless they are still used. It is interesting to note that numerous manufacturers prepare informational and operational sheets or charts as guides in the use of their products.

Instruction sheets actually came into prominence during the period when few or no textbooks were available. Whether or not they are to be continued as instructional aids in public schools is conjectural. Undoubtedly, the need for some types will diminish as more and better printed teaching materials become available.

In general, five kinds of instruction sheets are recognized. These are referred to as operation sheet, information sheet, job sheet, job plan, and assignment sheet. The purpose of this chapter is to describe these teaching devices and discuss briefly some of their advantages and limitations.

OPERATION SHEET

An operation sheet contains detailed instructions on how to perform a specific operation. It not only tells what is to be done, but describes

---

[1] R. W. Selvidge, *Individual Instruction Sheets* (Peoria, Ill.: Chas. A. Bennett Co., 1926).

120

Operation Sheet No. 15

How to Punch Holes with a Solid Punch[2]

The use of solid punches is generally limited to cutting small-diameter holes ranging from 3/32'' to 3/8'' in very light sheet metal. These punches are simply solid pieces of tool steel with small flat points (see Fig. 1). Here is how a solid punch should be used:

1. Mark the center of the hole to be punched lightly with a prick punch or center punch.

Fig. 1. Solid Punch

2. Place the metal on a lead block. In the absence of a lead block, use the end grain of a hardwood block. Do not use the flat face or cross-grain side of the wooden block, as the metal will bend when the punch is driven and the resulting hole is generally distorted. Never use a steel block as a supporting surface, as this will ruin the punch.

3. Select the correct punch and place it over the indentation mark. Hold the punch in a vertical position and strike it lightly with a hammer. Remove the punch and check to see if the punch is in the right location. Then strike the punch with a heavier blow (see Fig. 2). When striking the punch, watch the cutting point and not the head of the punch.

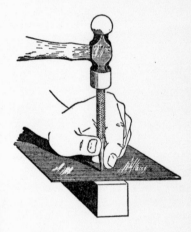

Fig. 2. Using Solid Punch

4. As a rule, the underside of the sheet where the hole is punched will bulge up slightly. Flatten the sheet by placing it on a smooth plate and striking it with a mallet (see Fig. 3).

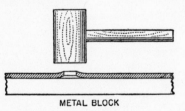

METAL BLOCK

Fig. 3. Flattening the Bulge with a Mallet

Fig. 24. Example of an Operation Sheet

[2] J. W. Giachino, *Basic Sheet Metal Practice* (Scranton: International Textbook Co., 1952).

how each step is to be carried out. In addition to written instructions, an operation sheet shows numerous illustrations of the various operating steps. The instructions are not for any particular job but describe the operation in such a way that it can be used on any job. With this type of instructional organization, a separate operation sheet for each operation included in the course of study is necessary. An example of an operation sheet is shown in Fig. 24.

INFORMATION SHEET

An information sheet is one which contains the pertinent information a student needs to know. This information may be of a general, technical, socioeconomic, safety, or occupational nature. The title of each information sheet is taken from the information topics listed in the course of study. A typical information sheet is illustrated on p. 123.

JOB SHEET

A job sheet is perhaps the most difficult type of instruction sheet to prepare and probably one having the least value in an instructional program. This sheet contains all the necessary directions for the completion of a job or project. It includes the tools and materials to be used and describes each operation which must be performed. Since the job or project may involve several operations, such a sheet must of necessity be unusually lengthy. For example, a job sheet may be prepared for building a birdhouse, or wiring an electric lamp. Inasmuch as each step of these jobs must be minutely described, the job sheet presents a great deal of written instructions. Moreover, if for one reason or another the instructor decides to eliminate the project from the instructional program, then the job sheet no longer would be of any value. Furthermore, the detailed instructions are often far too complex for most students to follow. The limitation of a job sheet becomes even more evident when its value is considered from the standpoint of student learning. The extensive instructions permit little or no student planning; the task simply becomes a problem of following directions.

Job sheets were highly regarded during the early era of vocational education when the exercise method of teaching predominated. By having a job sheet for each exercise, the complexity of teaching was thereby greatly simplified. The philosophy which characterizes vocational education today advocates considerable student planning and problem solving. The implementation of such a philosophy with the extensive use of job sheets is therefore questionable.

INFORMATION SHEET NO. 20
FITS, LIMITS AND TOLERANCES[3]

ALTHOUGH THE STUDENT in the average metalwork shop is not directly concerned with making parts which require precision fits, nevertheless, he should have an understanding and appreciation of their function and importance in industrial work. Mass production is possible because of this close attention to fits, which also insures the efficient operation and long-wearing qualities of the innumerable mechanical contrivances that are in existence today.

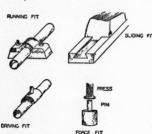

Fig. 1 Types of fits.

Machine Fits

There are five types of fits (see Fig. 1) used in machine- and toolwork: running fit, sliding fit, driving fit, force fit, and shrinkage fit. The *running fit* is employed when two parts must move freely, such as a shaft in a bearing. The *push* or *sliding fit* is one in which two surfaces are in contact with each other and must be movable when necessary, such as the tail stock on the bed of a lathe.

The driving, forced, and shrinkage fits are employed when two parts are to re-

main indefinitely in a fixed position. The *driving fit* is one in which the two sections are hammered together, such as driving a pin into a shaft. The *force fit* is one in which the two pieces are put together under pressure of a screw or hydraulic press. The *shrinkage fit*, as its name implies, is obtained by expanding the surface of the outside piece by means of heat and then inserting the unheated internal section. When the assembled piece is cooled, the shrinkage produced will result in locking the two parts together.

As a general rule, force and driving fits are used on work having small diameters and shrinkage fits on larger size pieces.

Limits and Tolerances

To insure a uniform degree of accuracy for all parts, the worker must perform various operations to meet definite specifications. The dimensions on the blueprint which guide the operator in carrying out

Fig. 2 Limits.

the job are known as basic dimensions. These, of course, represent an absolute perfect size of the finished piece. Since it is practically impossible to obtain such accuracy, the common practice is to show a range either above or below these basic

dimensions from which the operator is allowed to deviate. These restrictions are known as limits and are always shown on the blueprint either in the title block or on the dimension itself.

Fig. 2 illustrates a section that is to be cut 5″ in length, but an allowance of ±.005″ is permitted, meaning that the piece cannot be longer than 5.005″ or shorter than 4.995″. *Limits* can be said then to represent the extremes in size that are acceptable on a finished product. The difference

between the extreme is known as *tolerance*. Thus, in the example mentioned, the tolerance is .010″ and this is the distance or the leeway the worker can stray from the true dimensions.

QUESTIONS
1. What relation does precision work have to various types of fits?
2. What is the difference between a sliding and running fit?
3. How does a shrink fit differ from a forced fit?
4. What is meant by a driving fit?
5. What is meant by limits and tolerances?
6. How are limits expressed?

[3] J. W. Giachino and J. L. Feirer, *Basic Bench Metal Practice* (Peoria, Ill.: Chas. A. Bennett Co., 1943).

Job Plan No. 6

Sheet Metal Tool Box

(See print No. 6)

I. Tools and Machines

1. Rule	6. Soldering copper
2. Square	7. Cornice brake
3. Scriber	8. Rivet set
4. Hammer	9. Bar folder
5. Center punch	10. Snips

II. Material

1. 24-gauge galvanized iron
2. R.H. rivets 1/8'' in diameter
3. Wire solder

III. Procedure

1. Secure stock
2. Lay out pattern of box
3. Cut piece
4. Bend hem
5. Bend sides of box
6. Lay out tray and cut
7. Shape tray
8. Lay out handle
9. Form handle
10. Rivet sides of box
11. Solder tray to box
12. Fasten handle

Fig. 25. Example of a Job Plan

JOB PLAN

A job plan may be considered as a simplified form of a job sheet. Whereas a job sheet describes in considerable detail all the steps that are involved in the construction of a project, a job plan simply lists the essential performance steps without actually telling how the work is to be done. In other words, a job plan states what is to be accomplished without stipulating how it is to be carried out.

124

The chief advantage of a job plan is that the instructions are greatly simplified and, therefore, much easier to prepare. This type of instruction sheet is helpful to the teacher in starting a class, especially when many activities are to occur simultaneously. Its limitation, of course, is that it provides very little opportunity for student initiative or planning. Many teachers often employ these job plans during the early phases of the course work. Later, when the student has become more acclimated to shop or laboratory activities, he is permitted to use student planning sheets described in Chapter XVII. An example of a job plan is shown in Fig. 25. It provides a quick check, both for the teacher and the student of the tools, machines, materials, and procedures involved.

ASSIGNMENT SHEET

An assignment sheet contains written instructions to guide a student in studying, reading, or conducting investigations. The most common type of assignment sheet usually consists of a series of references to be read and questions to be answered. A more comprehensive kind of assignment sheet is often referred to as a student study guide. The nature and value of student study guides is discussed in more detail in Chapter XVII.

ADVANTAGES OF INSTRUCTION SHEETS

Written instruction sheets should always be regarded as only one of the many teaching techniques to be used in a shop or laboratory program. Undoubtedly, in some teaching situations a moderate use of instruction sheets probably is desirable. Often the nature of the learning activities may preclude the utilization of any instruction sheets. If a teacher finds that circumstances necessitate the preparation of instruction sheets, he should by all means make full use of them. Before launching forth on such a writing task, he should first of all ascertain if similar information may be secured in printed form. If the material is available, it is often better to adopt it rather than to spend endless hours duplicating it. An important consideration in the preparation of instruction sheets is the ability of the teacher to write. Unless he can do a credible job, he should not attempt to place material in the hands of students that may be subject to criticism. Too often in the past a teacher has been severely censured for the abominably poor instructional sheets which he has produced. Generally speaking, the following may be considered to be the significant advantages of instruction sheets:

1. They provide for individualized instruction. Instruction sheets allow each student to progress at his own rate of learning.

2. They are extremely helpful in handling large classes where it is almost impossible for the teacher to give attention to individual needs.

3. They help students recall demonstrations. In a multiactivity type of shop it is very difficult to present demonstrations and information lessons at a time when the majority of students need them. Since there is often a lapse of time between the presentation of a lesson and its application, instructions may be partially forgotten. The availability of instruction sheets will therefore help students recall the needed information.

4. They serve a useful purpose when adequate instructional material cannot be obtained in printed form.

5. They make it possible for the teacher to spend more time supervising the work of individual students.

LIMITATIONS OF INSTRUCTION SHEETS

Instruction sheets have several rather serious limitations. Specifically these are:

1. It is difficult to prepare good instruction sheets. To be effective, such sheets not only must be stated in explicit language but they should be profusely illustrated.

2. Mimeographed instructions are never as appealing to students as printed ones.

3. Teachers with a teaching plan based on instruction sheets may come to depend entirely on the written sheets rather than on some other methods of teaching.

4. The individual student's growth becomes dependent largely on his reading ability, or more psychologically upon his development in verbalization.

5. They do not permit individual planning.

6. They hinder group planning and co-operative endeavor.

7. They tend to promote a definite pattern of instruction. Once a teacher has developed a set of instruction sheets, he is not inclined to discard them. Accordingly, there is danger that the same projects are repeated year after year.

DISCUSSION QUESTIONS

1. What is an operation sheet?
2. What are some of the advantages and limitations of operation sheets in an instruction program?
3. What is meant by an information sheet?
4. Of what particular value are information sheets?
5. When is a teacher justified in writing information sheets?
6. How does a job sheet differ from an operation sheet?
7. What are some of the main objections to the use of job sheets?
8. In what way does a job plan differ from a job sheet?
9. Should a teacher use job plans? Why?
10. What is meant by an assignment sheet?
11. Is a teacher justified in saying that all instruction sheets have little educational value in a teaching program? Why?
12. Cite some of the conditions when instruction sheets would prove valuable as teaching aids?

SPECIAL ASSIGNMENT

Prepare one of the following instruction sheets: operation sheet, information sheet, job sheet, job plan.

ADDITIONAL READING

Ericson, E. E., *Teaching the Industrial Arts* (Peoria, Ill.: Chas. A. Bennett Co., 1946), pp. 54–62.

Selvidge, R. W., *Individual Instruction Sheets* (Peoria, Ill.: Chas. A. Bennett Co., 1926).

Struck, F. T., *Creative Teaching* (New York: John Wiley & Sons, Inc., 1938), pp. 371–394.

Wilber, G. O., *Industrial Arts in General Education* (Scranton, Pa.: The International Textbook Co., 1949), pp. 155–179.

CHAPTER 16————

Student Planning

All types of industrial arts and vocational education work should provide for some student planning. Insofar as pupil growth is concerned, more educational value is often derived through the process of student planning than in the acquisition of factual knowledge or completion of manipulative work assignments. Student planning is a concrete method of teaching students to analyze, organize and appraise learning experiences. Too often in the past, the instructional program has been limited to the completion of so many projects or jobs and learning a specified quantity of related information.

An organization whereby students are encouraged to plan their work undoubtedly is much more difficult to execute. Consequently, some teachers have hesitated to adopt such a teaching plan. Others have rejected the idea, believing that students are too immature and lack the necessary background to plan work effectively. In spite of the protest of some teachers, student planning has proved successful whenever it has been used properly.

Student planning consists of two main stages of activity—project designing and preparing a work plan. Each of these phases will be discussed in this chapter.

PLANNING THE PROJECT

In a real functional shop or laboratory program, especially on an industrial arts level, a student should have some voice in the type of project which he is to make. As it was indicated in Chapter XI, the selection of projects should be under the guidance of the teacher in order to insure maximum participation in purposeful learning. However, the fact remains that a student should have the opportunity to work on projects which have special values and which appeal to him. Accordingly, the first step in student planning is to make certain that a proper choice of project has been made. The teacher should make source materials available, that is, textbooks, magazines, and other literature containing suggestions for projects. Once an agreement has been reached as to the appropriate project to be made, then the teacher should require each student to make a complete working drawing. This drawing need not be a finished mechanical type of drawing; usually a freehand sketch is adequate. However, the sketch should be complete insofar as views and dimensions are concerned. Sketching the project is usually simplified if it is produced on some form of cross-section or graph paper.

During the process of sketching the project, the student should be encouraged to incorporate his own ideas, especially in regard to the shape, size, and other design features so that the completed project actually represents his own creation and meets all the specifications of his needs. One very important responsibility of the teacher during this stage of the planning is to check carefully the sketch after it is completed. A student should never be allowed to start construction until the teacher has approved the sketch.

PLANNING THE WORK PROCEDURE

The real educative value of student planning is manifested in the process which he employs to analyze the construction details of the project. Here a student has to make decisions as to what tools and equipment he will need, what kind and quantity of materials to use, and what steps are to be followed in making the project. To simplify the execution of this part of the work, the teacher should provide the student with some planning form. Usually, this form consists of blank spaces where the student fills in the required details of his work plan. A typical student planning sheet is shown in Fig. 26. Regardless of the format used, it is important to keep the planning sheet as simple as possible. A complicated form not only loses its appeal to the student but it becomes extremely difficult for the teacher to check.

In general, a student planning sheet should be divided into four main parts. One section should require such data as the name of the project, student's name, grade level, and name of the course. There should be a blank where the instructor can place his O.K. of the plan, and spaces to

Student Planning Sheet

Section I

Name of Project _____

Student name _____   Date started _____

Grade level _____   Date completed _____

Course _____   Instructor's grade _____

Instructor's O.K. _____   Student's grade _____

Section II

Tools and Machines I Will Use

1. _____   6. _____

2. _____   7. _____

3. _____   8. _____

4. _____   9. _____

5. _____   10. _____

Section III

Material I Will Need

No. Pieces	Description of Material	Size	Cost
		Total Cost	

Section IV

How I Plan To Make My Project

1. _____
2. _____
3. _____
4. _____
5. _____
6. _____
7. _____
8. _____
9. _____
10. _____
11. _____
12. _____
13. _____
14. _____

Fig. 26. Typical Planning Sheet Giving Details of Student's Work Plan

record the date when the project was started and when it was completed, and the grade received for the completed work.

Another section of the planning sheet should provide blanks where the student can enter the tools and machines he intends to use.

The third section of the plan should contain provisions for listing the quantity and kinds of materials to be used. It is advisable in this section to provide a column for entering the cost of the materials. Determining costs is a valuable part of student learning and this computation is especially helpful if the student must pay for the supplies.

The fourth section is probably the most difficult for beginning students to complete. Here the student must specify the sequence of the operations that are to be performed. The student will have to analyze carefully his working drawing and then write down each step he intends to follow in fabricating the project.

TEACHING STUDENTS TO PLAN

The actual process of student planning must be taught. It is inconceivable to expect a student to prepare worth-while plans unless he has been properly orientated in the techniques of planning.

Inasmuch as the first phase of planning involves the preparation of a working drawing, the teacher must at the offset determine whether or not a student has an understanding of freehand sketching or mechanical drafting. Lacking this skill, the teacher's first responsibility is to teach the student the basic elements of sketching.

In undertaking the teaching of the actual project-planning process, one plan which may be used is to take some simple project and have the entire class carry out each step of the planning together. For example, the teacher might display a working model of a project or have a working drawing of the project on the blackboard. After pointing out some of the features of this project, the teacher then proceeds to ask the students what tools and machines are necessary for making it. As a tool or machine is mentioned, the teacher should write it down on the blackboard. An alternative method is to provide each student with a planning sheet and, as the tools are mentioned, to have everyone write the name in the blanks provided. Once the list of tools and equipment is completed, the teacher then raises questions as to the steps that are involved in constructing the project. As each operation is mentioned, the teacher should discuss the appropriateness of the operation and its logical order of sequence. By taking the students through this entire planning, they will develop the necessary understanding of what is expected. With some groups it may be necessary to repeat this process several times, either with the class as a group or on an individual basis.

Another equally successful method when teaching students to plan a project is to have them fill out one section at a time of the planning sheet. Thus, for their first project, the planning may be limited to recording the tools and machines. For their second project they may be taught how to make out a bill of material. Finally, for their third project, they may be required to work out the construction procedure and perhaps even be given an opportunity to appraise their finished product.

CHECKING THE PLAN

As mentioned previously, it is very important that the teacher check each plan before allowing the student to begin work. If this is not done, there is likely to occur considerable wastage of materials, improper execution of operations, hazardous working conditions and, above all, possible failure to complete the work. Therefore, the instructor should make it a point to sit down with each student and discuss the merits and limitations of his plan. Such a session is especially valuable because the teacher can use this occasion to have the student justify questionable aspects of the plan. It also permits an opportunity for the teacher to commend the student, to suggest alternate working methods, and to stimulate the student to continue further analytical generalizations.

STUDENT EVALUATION

It is a foregone conclusion that all student work must be evaluated. Most teachers usually assume complete responsibility for this grading. However, current educational philosophy now recognizes that some student appraisal is a valuable aspect of an instructional program. A student, to arrive at an equitable appraisal of his work, must have some specific evaluation criteria. Perhaps this criteria can be worked out with the entire class or the teacher may simply set up certain specifications of workmanship. Regardless of the method used, it is important that certain evaluation factors be established. A student, then, is in a position to pass judgment on his work. For example, tests of workmanship for a low-voltage d.c. motor might read as follows:

1. Does the motor run?
2. Are all coils wound carefully with each following closely behind the one preceding it? Are all coils insulated and varnished?
3. Is the armature well balanced?
4. Is the commutator concentric with the rotor shaft?

5. Is there a minimum of clearance between the armature magnets and the field magnets?
6. Are all the bends on the metal done neatly?
7. Are all body and base parts neatly and properly finished?

To arrive at an evaluation of this project, the student might conclude that:

1. The motor runs, but not as fast as Jim Smith's. I think it is because my commutator is not centered properly.
2. The coils are wound correctly according to the teacher's instructions.
3. The armature is well balanced, but the commutator wobbles.
4. The armature magnets run very close to the field magnets.
5. The metal work is well done, neat and good looking. Everything is well finished. It is an excellent motor with the exception of the wobbly commutator.

In preparing an evaluation scale, each accepted standard might be given a specific value. With such a rating scale, the student's task of evaluation is further simplified. Moreover, it permits him to establish the grade on a much more objective basis.

Given an opportunity, most students will make an honest appraisal of their work. Usually, they are inclined to grade themselves too low rather than too high. Actually, it is not the grade that is particularly significant. Of even greater value is the experience students receive in passing judgment on the quality of their work.

DISCUSSION QUESTIONS

1. What are some of the educational values that result when students are given an opportunity to plan their work?
2. Why do some teachers object to student planning? Is this viewpoint justifiable? Explain.
3. What type of a drawing should a student have before undertaking construction of his project?
4. How should a teacher go about encouraging students to design their own projects?
5. In planning the work procedure, why should a teacher provide some form of planning sheet?
6. Why should a planning sheet be very simple?
7. What are some of the items that should be included in a student planning sheet.
8. Why is it important for the teacher to actually teach students how to plan?
9. How would you proceed to teach students how to plan their work?

10. Why is it extremely important for the teacher to check each plan before allowing students to work on their project.
11. In working out a plan for a project, if a student should deviate from what might be standard practice, what point of view should the teacher take?
12. Why should students be given an opportunity to appraise their work?

ADDITIONAL READING

Friese, John F., "Recording and Weighting Industrial-Arts Grades," *Industrial Arts and Vocational Education*, June, 1949, p. 223.

Garlak, Frank J., "Grading the Shop Student," *Industrial Arts and Vocational Education*, June, 1946, p. 254.

Johnsen, M. O., "A Method in Grading Shop Projects in Metalwork," *Industrial Arts and Vocational Education*, April, 1950, p. 154.

Lush, Clifford, "A Student Rating Scale," *School Shop*, Feb. 1948, p. 19.

Struck, F. T., *Creative Teaching* (New York: John Wiley & Sons, Inc., 1938), pp. 302–323.

Vaughn and Mays, *Content and Methods of the Industrial Arts* (New York: The Century Co., 1924), pp. 105–122.

Wilber, G. O., *Industrial Arts in General Education* (Scranton, Pa.: The Industrial Textbook Co., 1949), pp. 181–193.

CHAPTER 17 —————————

Student Study Guides

In many respects a student study guide is comparable to the assignment sheet mentioned in Chapter XV. However, a study guide has certain other ramifications which makes it unique in itself. Primarily, its function is to assist students to study, to read, or to investigate various categories of information, problems, or manipulative activities. The material in this chapter deals with a description of study guides and their value in an instructional program.

TYPES OF STUDY GUIDES

Study guides may be divided into three main groups, namely, informational, investigatory, and manipulative. The informational study guide is designed to help a student seek certain kinds of information which are essential to the basic comprehension of the course. The investigatory type of study guide is intended to assist a student perform an experiment or undertake a simple research problem. The manipulative study guide is used (1) to help a pupil study the necessary operations to be performed in constructing a project, and (2) to give him the essential instructions in starting his project.

Although study guides may be prepared on the basis of the three mentioned functions, it is often more convenient to combine two of them, that is, to have one guide deal with both informational and manipulative activities. However, the identity and scope of the assignment is relatively unimportant; the essential consideration is the availability of guides that will serve their intended purpose, namely, direct student learning.

ESSENTIAL PARTS OF A STUDY GUIDE

A study guide should contain the following four parts: purpose, study questions, references, and practical application.

The purpose should state the specific objective of the assignment in terms of what the student is expected to learn. Thus, the assignment may involve the application of a wood finish. The statement may then be expressed somewhat as follows: "The purpose of this assignment is to give you an opportunity to learn how to apply a varnish finish."

Under the heading "Study Questions" there should be listed a series of pertinent questions designed especially to guide the student's reading. These questions may later be used as main points for a class discussion. Very often, instead of having questions requiring an essay type of answer, there may be substituted an objective kind of items such as true and false, completion, multiple choice, etc.

The reference section should present all the available sources where the student may find the information needed to answer the listed questions. The title of each book or periodical should be accurately stated and the exact pages shown where the information is to be found.

The last part, labeled "Practical Application," should include one or more specific tasks involving an application of the material read. If the study guide is centered around an informational topic, the practical application may consist of a few problems which actually test a student's understanding of the assigned material. For a manipulative study guide there may be listed several projects from which a student may select the one he wishes to make, and some concrete instructions concerning the planning and construction of this project. A study of the three sample study guides shown in Figs. 27, 28, and 29 will illustrate more clearly the nature of the material to be included in the practical application section.

VALUES OF STUDY GUIDES

One of the basic principles of good learning is that the student should have a clear picture of the experiences in which he is to participate. He should be able to see the relationship of the various lessons and how they fit into the course as a whole. Too often the teacher unfolds the course lesson by lesson and the student may never realize the real significance of the relationship between these lessons and the objectives established for the course. Sometimes the teacher attempts to achieve this general understanding by means of a brief orientation lesson at the beginning of the course. During this period, he probably presents the

Assignment No. 2

Making a Layout

I. Purpose

The purpose of this assignment is to give you an opportunity to learn how to make a layout directly on metal stock.

II. Study Questions

1. Why must a layout be very accurate?

2. How does the use of layout fluid help make a layout more accurate?

3. What is the function of center lines for a layout?

4. If the edge of the stock is to be the starting point of the layout, why should this edge be absolutely straight?

5. Why should the center be lightly prick-punched before scribing the arc?

6. Why should centers for all holes be located by two intersecting lines?

7. How do dividers differ from a compass?

8. Why is a protractor head used for drawing angular lines?

9. What are the functions of bending lines?

References

1. Giachino, J.W., and Feirer, J. L., Basic Bench-Metal Practice (Peoria, Ill. 1943), Chas. A. Bennett Co., pp. 30-32.
2. Tustison, F. E., and Kranzusch, R. F., Metalwork Essentials, The Bruce Publishing Co., 1936: pp. 7-12.

Practical Applications

1. Of the projects listed below, select the one which you would like to make.

 a) Towel rack
 b) Table lamp
 c) Smoking stand
 d) Flower pot hanger

2. Check with the instructor for a print of the project selected.

3. Make a working drawing of your project.

4. Fill out a student planning sheet.

Fig. 27. Example No. 1 of Informational Type of Student Study Guide

Assignment No. 1

Metals Used in Sheet-Metal Work

I. Purpose

A variety of metals are used in a sheet-metal shop, such as black iron, galvanized iron, copper sheet, tin plate, terne plate, aluminum, and stainless steel. The purpose of this assignment is to give you an opportunity to learn some of the general characteristics of these metals.

II. Study Questions

1. For what type of work is black-iron sheet used?

2. Galvanized iron is coated with what kind of material?

3. What particular quality does galvanized iron have?

4. What are some of the common uses of galvanized iron?

5. What advantage do the nonflaking sheets have over the standard galvanized sheets?

6. What is tin plate?

7. What are some of the common uses of tin plate?

8. What is the difference between coke and charcoal tin plate?

9. How are charcoal plates graduated?

10. How is tin plate sold?

11. What is terne plate?

12. Why should terne plate never be used to make containers that are to hold food?

13. For what purpose is sheet copper used in the building industry?

14. What are some of the advantages of aluminum over other types of sheet metal?

15. What is the difference between heat-treatable aluminum and nonheat-treatable aluminum?

16. How are the hardnesses of nonheat-treatable aluminum indicated?

17. What particular advantage does stainless steel have over other metals?

18. Why is stainless steel more difficult to form?

III. References

1. Giachino, J.W., Basic Sheet Metal Practice, (Scranton, Pa. 1952), International Textbook Co., pp. 1-8.
2. Bruce, L. F., Sheet Metal, (Chicago: American Technical Society, 1951), pp. 27-33.

IV. Practical Applications

1. What is the cost of a sheet of No. 28-gage galvanized iron that is 30" wide and 96" long, if the price is 20 cents per pound?

2. Determine the amount of aluminum you will need to make a box 30" high, and 36" long.

Fig. 28. Example No. 2 of Informational Type of Student Study Guide

Assignment No. 10

Opportunities in Woodwork

I. Purpose

The purpose of this assignment is to give you an opportunity to investigate some of the common woodworking occupations.

II. Study Questions

For each of the occupations listed below, find out what the worker does.

OCCUPATION	WHAT HE DOES
A. Carpenter	
B. Cabinetmaker	
C. Patternmaker	
D. Forester	

III. References

1. Feirer, J.L. Industrial Arts Woodworking, Peoria, Ill., Chas. A. Bennett Co., 1950, pp 242-244.
2. Michigan Unemployment Compensation Commission, Woodworking Occupations, Detroit, 1950.
3. U.S. Dept. of Labor, Occupational Outlook Handbook, Washington, D.C., 1951, pp. 284-292.

IV. Practical Application

1. Select some woodworking occupation.

2. Visit a person who is working at this particular occupation and ask him about the items listed below. If you cannot find someone working at this trade, ask the librarian for material containing information on woodworking occupations.

3. Write a report of your findings and make arrangements with your teacher to present the report to the class.

4. Information which you are to secure for the occupation selected:

   a) Specific type of work that is done
   b) Kind of skills that are necessary to do this work
   c) Length of training required to acquire the skills
   d) Rate of pay
   e) Job opportunities in this type of work
   f) Amount of formal education required

Fig. 29. Example of Investigative Type of Student Study Guide

139

main objectives of the course and explains how these objectives are to be attained. He may also discuss the nature of the work which students will be expected to complete and other specific course requirements. Although such a practice is highly desirable, it has one limitation. Students too often either fail to grasp the true implication of the stated "over-all course view" or they quickly foregt it. The use of study guides will facilitate a more comprehensive understanding of the work they are to do, because it places in their hands constant reminders of the general scope of the course. They have before them, parenthetically speaking, a visual device which shows where they start, where they are going, and where they should arrive.

A second value of study guides is that they help students study more effectively. One of the most difficult problems of students is to discriminate between what really is significant and what is unimportant. Study guides, when properly designed, will assist materially in increasing the efficiency of student learning, since the teacher has taken the necessary precautions to channel study in the right direction.

A third value of study guides is that they are extremely helpful in managing a shop or laboratory in which numerous activities are occurring simultaneously. Many teachers are always confronted with the problem of getting different groups started at the same time, or in supervising the work of students when they are all engaged in different activities. Problems of this nature are greatly reduced if study guides are used. For example, while the teacher is demonstrating to one group, the other students may be working on their assignments. In this manner everyone has a task and the teacher is freed of annoyances which generally prevail when students are idly standing by waiting for instructions.

A fourth value of study guides is that they establish a definite understanding of what the students are expected to accomplish while enrolled in the course. Each student knows from the very beginning exactly how much work he must accomplish. In other words, it places more responsibility on the students for meeting the requirements which the teacher has specified for the course.

THE TEXTBOOK

To a large extent the textbook can be considered a study guide, especially if it is used under proper teacher guidance. Some teachers, however, are inclined to minimize the importance of the textbook for shop-work. These people are of the opinion that, since a shop or laboratory course deals primarily with manipulative activities, a book is not particularly valuable. They feel that whatever instructions a student needs, the teacher is best qualified to render them.

The practice of another group of teachers is to place several different volumes on a shelf and a student is referred to them when the occasion demands it. Then again, other teachers find it more expedient to adopt a basic text for each course, and every student is required to possess a copy.

Although circumstances may influence the method of using textbooks in a particular teaching situation, the following generalizations are worthy of consideration:

1. By and large, a textbook is looked upon as an indispensable tool of learning for academic courses. Shop or laboratory work, if it is to provide rich and varied experiences, should involve more than just manipulative activities. Many learning experiences are possible only through the medium of textbooks. Accordingly, it seems reasonable to assume that a text for manipulative work is probably as important as it is for any other course.

2. The use of textbooks gives the shop and laboratory course a certain degree of respectability. Since many people view textbooks and education as being almost synonymous, more prestige is attached to a manipulative type of course if a text is used. The teacher can more easily create an atmosphere that, in shop or laboratory work, certain types of practical experiences are rendered, but, in addition, comparable learning opportunities are provided, as may be characteristic of any other academic course.

3. Students like textbooks. Contrary to the belief of some people, the majority of students prefer to have a basic text for a course. In fact, they are much more receptive to using a text than if they were limited to the few available books in the shop or having to go to the library. The implication is not that students should be discouraged from consulting many sources of information or going to the library. The fact remains that to students the text is a convenient means of learning.

4. Teachers who use few or no textbooks maintain that textbooks are not particularly suitable for their course. Perhaps there is no such thing as the perfect text for any given course, nevertheless, it is far better to have one that fits the course reasonably well than to deprive students of the experiences generally associated with textbooks.

5. Textbooks are valuable teaching aids, especially if no other written instructional material is available. They not only permit the teacher to devote more time to actual instruction but, in addition, they serve as

a check on the scope of work to be covered in a course. Textbooks also enable the students to study certain materials before a demonstration is presented, and give them an opportunity to follow up oral instructions. They conserve the teacher's time because the students can be placed on their own resources in acquiring material to be learned. Finally, lacking instruction sheets or study guides, textbooks will simplify the task of handling large classes.

6. Textbooks provide practice in reading. Schools are often accused of turning out people who cannot comprehend printed instructions. The industrial arts and vocational education teacher should not cast off his responsibility of teaching pupils to read by saying that this is the function of the English teacher. It is just as important for the shop and laboratory teacher to teach his students to read technical material, as it is the responsibility of the English teacher, the mathematics teacher, or any other teacher on the staff.

DISCUSSION QUESTIONS

1. What is the general purpose of student study guides?
2. Explain the function of the various types of guides.
3. What kind of material should be included in study guides?
4. What are some of the specific values of study guides?
5. How does a study guide differ from the conventional type of assignment sheet?
6. Why should textbooks be considered as a form of study guide?
7. Why are some instructors reluctant to use textbooks?
8. What are some of the reasons why textbooks should be used in shopwork?

SPECIAL ASSIGNMENT

Prepare one student study guide.

ADDITIONAL READING

Ericson, E. E., *Teaching the Industrial Arts* (Peoria, Ill.: Chas. A. Bennett Co., 1946), pp. 148–160.

Smith, Homer J., "A Defense of Textbooks," *Industrial Arts and Vocational Education*, April, 1932, p. 21.

Struck, F. T., *Creative Teaching* (New York: John Wiley and Sons, 1938), chaps. VII, XVII.

Wilson, J. Douglas, "Textbook Utilization," *Industrial Arts and Vocational Education*, April, 1951, p. 140.

Williams, Amos G., "Choosing Your Textbook," *Industrial Arts and Vocational Education*, October, 1945, p. 34.

Wyman, William T., "The Selection of Textbooks for Vocational Schools," *Industrial Arts and Vocational Education*, October, 1932, p. 21.

Yoakam, G. A., *The Improvement of the Assignment* (New York: Macmillan, 1932), pp. 246–263.

INDEX

A

Agricultural education, 17, 18
  Adult farmer classes, 18
  Classes for young farmers, 17, 18
All-day classes
  Agriculture, 17
  Homemaking, 18, 19
  Trade, 14, 15
Analysis, instructional, 68
Analyzing course of study, 72–77
Analyzing operations, 102–104
Analyzing related information, 105–107
Arranging operations, 78–85
  Instructional chart, 81–85
  Production, 80, 81
  Servicing, 79, 80
Assignment sheet, 125
Auxiliary knowledge, 97, 103

B

Blocks, 69
Bollinger, 72

C

Campbell, 3
Caswell, 3
Chart form, examples, 83, 84
Course objectives, 61–66
  Examples, 64–66
  Misconceptions, 61, 62
  Preparing, 61–63
  Selecting, 62
Course of study
  Arranging operations, 78–85
  Assembling, 109–118
  Importance, 4
  Listing projects, 92, 93
  Main divisions, 68–70
  Need for revision, 5
  Parts, 7
  Related information, 95–100
  Selecting operations, 72–77
  Subdivisions, 70
Course of study formats, 113, 114
Course outline, 7
  Examples, 8–11
Curriculum, 1–3

D

Day-unit class, agriculture, 17
Demonstration, 36
Diamond, 42
Distributive education, 19
Distributive occupations, 19

Diversified occupations, 16, 19
Douglass, 6

E

Education, general, 12
Educational philosophy, 23
  Developing, 48–59
  Meaning, 49
  Preparing statement, 57
Educational policies commission, 52
Ericson, 3, 6
Evening trade extension, 15

F

Fales, 13
Federally reimbursed programs, 14
Friese, 62
Fryklund, 72, 97

G

General education
  Definition, 12, 13
  Philosophy, 49, 50
General information, 95, 96
  Arranging, 98, 99
  Identifying, 97, 98
  Selecting, 98
Grading, 40, 41, 46

H

Homemaking education, 18
  Type of classes, 18, 19

I

Imperative educational needs of youth, 49
Individual differences
  Providing for, 37–38, 44
Industrial arts
  Definition, 13
  Objectives, 53
  Philosophy, 50–53
Industrial education, 17
Information lesson, 102
Information sheet, 123
Instruction sheets, 120–126
  Advantages, 125, 126
  Limitations, 126
Instructional aids, 37, 43
Instructional analysis, 68–71
  Function, 68
Instructional plan
  Basic elements, 1
Instructional practices
  Examples, 43–46
  Preparing plan, 35–42

Introductory statement, 28–30
  Samples, 31–33

J

Job, 76, 87–93
Job plan, 124
Job sheet, 122

K

Krug, 62

L

Lesson, 102
Lesson plan, 102

O

Objectives, 23
  Industrial arts, 53
  Misconceptions, 61, 62
  Selecting, 62
  Vocational education, 56
Occupational information, 97
Operations
  Analyzing, 102–104
  Arranging, 78–85
  Designating, 74
  Identifying, 74, 75
  Listing, 76, 77
  Meaning, 72, 73
  Production, 73
  Servicing, 73
Operation sheet, 120, 121

P

Part-time classes, 15
  Agriculture, 17
  Business, 19
  Homemaking, 18
  Trade, 15
Part-time general continuation, 16
Part-time trade extension, 16
Part-time trade preparatory, 16
Performing steps, 103
Philosophy of industrial arts, 50–53
Philosophy of vocational education, 54–56
Planning projects, 128, 129
Practical arts
  Definition, 13
Principles of learning, 23–26
Production operation, 73
Program of studies, 1, 2
Projects, 87–93
  Production, 89, 90
  Selection, 90, 91
  Student selection, 91, 92

R

Records, shop, 42
Reeder, 3

Related information, 95–100
  Analyzing, 105–107
  Kinds, 95
Related subjects, 97

S

Safety, 41, 42
Safety information, 96, 97
Selvidge, 120
Service jobs, 87, 89
Servicing operation, 73
Shop finances, 40
Skill lesson, 102
Socio-economic information, 96
Struck, 54
Student evaluation, 132, 133
Student outcomes, 63
  Examples, 64–66
Student personnel organization, 38, 39, 44–45
Student planning, 39, 40, 45, 128–133
Student planning sheet, 130
Student study guides, 135–150
  Examples, 137–139
  Parts, 136
  Types, 135
  Values, 136

T

Teaching techniques, 26, 36, 43
Technical information, 96
Testing and grading, 40, 41, 46
Textbooks, 140–142
Trade and industrial education, 14
  Type of classes, 15, 16

U

Unit of instruction, 115, 116
Unit trade course, 15

V

Vehicles of instruction, 76
Vocational-agricultural education, 17
  Types of classes, 17, 18
Vocational-business education, 19
Vocational education
  Definition, 14
  Philosophy, 54–56
Vocational-homemaking education, 18
  Type of classes, 18, 19
Vocational-industrial education
  Definition, 14
  Type of classes, 15, 16
Vocational-technical education, 16

W

Weaver, 5
Wilber, 61
Work jobs
  Selection, 87–93